NATURE
PLAY
WORKSHOP
FOR FAMILIES

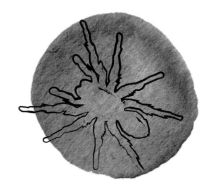

NATURE PLAY WORKSHOP

FOR FAMILIES

A GUIDE TO **40+** OUTDOOR LEARNING
EXPERIENCES IN **ALL SEASONS**

MONICA WIEDEL-LUBINSKI
& KAREN MADIGAN

Inspiring | Educating | Creating | Entertaining

Brimming with creative inspiration, how-to projects, and useful information to enrich your everyday life, Quarto Knows is a favorite destination for those pursuing their interests and passions. Visit our site and dig deeper with our books into your area of interest: Quarto Creates, Quarto Cooks, Quarto Homes, Quarto Lives, Quarto Drives, Quarto Explores, Quarto Gifts, or Quarto Kids.

First Published in 2020 by Quarry Books, an imprint of The Quarto Group, 100 Cummings Center, Suite 265-D, Beverly, MA 01915, USA. T (978) 282-9590 F (978) 283-2742 QuartoKnows.com

Quarry Books titles are also available at discount for retail, wholesale, promotional, and bulk purchase. For details, contact the Special Sales Manager by email at specialsales@quarto.com or by mail at The Quarto Group, Attn: Special Sales Manager, 100 Cummings Center, Suite 265-D, Beverly, MA 01915, USA.

10 9 8 7 6 5 4 3 2 1

ISBN: 978-1-63159-868-5

Digital edition published in 2020
eISBN: 978-1-63159-869-2

Library of Congress Cataloging-in-Publication Data

Names: Wiedel-Lubinski, Monica, author. | Madigan, Karen, author.
Title: Nature play workshop for families : a guide to 40+ outdoor learning
   experiences in all seasons / Monica Wiedel-Lubinski and Karen Madigan.
Description: Beverly, MA, USA : Quarry Publishing Group USA Inc., 2020. |
   Includes bibliographical references and index. | Audience: Ages 8-12 |
   Audience: Grades 4-6
Identifiers: LCCN 2020010706 (print) | LCCN 2020010707 (ebook) | ISBN
   9781631598685 (trade paperback) | ISBN 9781631598692 (ebook)
Subjects: LCSH: Family recreation. | Outdoor recreation. | Nature. | Games.
Classification: LCC GV182.8 .W554 2020 (print) | LCC GV182.8 (ebook) |
   DDC 790.1/91--dc23
LC record available at https://lccn.loc.gov/2020010706
LC ebook record available at https://lccn.loc.gov/2020010707

Design, page layout, and illustrations: Mattie Wells
Photography: Monica Berg except as follows
   Bill Bramble, pages 28, 30, 76 (top), and 94; Monica Wiedel-Lubinski pages 12, 47, 56, 57 (middle), 63 (top, middle), 67 (middle), 109 (bottom), and 114 (bottom left); Victoria Rose Brusaferro, page 98; Megan Long, page 117; and Shutterstock, pages 7 (last three images), 13, 18 (bottom left), 20, 23 (bottom), 24, 25 (top, bottom), 26, 35 (top, bottom), 37 (middle, bottom), 38 (top, bottom left), 40, 50, 54, 55 (middle, bottom), 57 (top, bottom), 58 (top, bottom left, bottom right), 60, 64, 65 (top), 66, 67 (top), 68, 69, 72, 73 (middle, bottom), 74, 75 (top, bottom), 76 (bottom row), 78, 79 (top, bottom), 80, 82, 83 (top), 91–93, 95 (top, middle), 96 (bottom row), 101 (top, button), 104, 105 (bottom), 106, 108, 110, 111, 114 (top, bottom middle, bottom right), 116, 117, 120, 128, 142

Printed in China

ACKNOWLEDGMENTS AND GRATITUDE

Over the years, our families, friends, and countless little children have inspired us to love others, and nature, more fully. We carry your love and wonder with us on every outdoor adventure.

We are grateful to talented photographer Monica Berg, whose images gracefully capture nature play throughout the book, and photographer Bill Bramble who contributed stunning nature photographs. We also thank the families and children who made time to be photographed, especially from Wild Haven Forest Preschool and A World of Friends School in Baltimore, Maryland.

To Dr. Mary Rivkin and all our colleagues who contributed insights, we appreciate your diverse perspectives on nature-based education. We deeply admire your dedication and expertise—thank you for freely sharing it with our readers.

To Cromwell Valley Park and Oregon Ridge Nature Center, we thank you for welcoming us into your wild spaces. We are especially grateful to Irvine Nature Center, where we established a nature preschool as colleagues and became dear friends.

ADDITIONAL WORDS OF GRATITUDE FROM MONICA

To Nick and my children, Ethan and Tessa, my heart couldn't be more full of gratitude for your love and support. From blueberry-picking days to firefly-catching nights and every wild moment in between, I am inspired by you. To my parents, thank you for sharing your love of gardening, spiders, and bees with me and for allowing me to climb the maple tree. To my sisters, extended family, and friends, thank you for grounding me with unshakable roots and constant encouragement.

ADDITIONAL WORDS OF GRATITUDE FROM KAREN

To my dear friends and family who have been there cheering me on, thank you. To my niece, Charley, who brings tremendous joy to our family, you inspire everyone around you to follow their hearts. To Tim, my best friend and husband, who shares my passion for nature, thank you for being by my side for every adventure. And to my lovable lab, Saint, I'm grateful that you cozied up next to me as I typed away; you are a true companion.

CONTENTS

1

SEASONAL NATURE PLAY: SUMMER

2

SEASONAL NATURE PLAY: AUTUMN

3

SEASONAL NATURE PLAY: WINTER

4

SEASONAL NATURE PLAY: SPRING

5

YEAR–ROUND NATURE PLAY

7

TEMPLATES

6

VOICES FROM THE FIELD

FOREWORD

Mary Rivkin, PhD

"It's such a nice day! Let's get the kids outside. Do something fun as a family!"

If you have ever said this or something like it, isn't the next sentence about what to do? You start to think what is possible, where is possible, and what is needed besides snacks. Maybe you grew up without playing outdoors much or in a different area where the outdoors had different things to do. This book can help you with what's next.

Monica Wiedel-Lubinski and Karen Madigan are seasoned outdoor teachers of young and elementary children. They have a strong understanding of what the outdoors offers to children for play and interest, and how adults and children can enjoy nature activities together. They also know that in the last 100 years or so, children have had increasingly less time outdoors, and firsthand knowledge about nature has decreased. Thus, parents and children are often beginners together in their nature explorations. This is particularly true in our migratory society, where contemporary families often live far from landscapes familiar to the adults. I observe my son, from Maryland's well-watered green fields and forests, now appreciating the subtle shades of olive, brown, and gray in the shrubs and grasses on the stony hillsides of Southern California. He and his three-year-old child roam trails and meadows, day by day making this their "home" country. "Hear that owl?" one will ask. Or "Where did the tadpoles go?" Child and father are learning together about this rich natural environment.

The authors' extensive teaching experiences are rooted in the mid-Atlantic states, and their deep array of activities reflect this background. Colleagues from other places also have contributed to the array. Every activity has been tested, tried numerous times, enjoyed, and found practical. Not every activity is doable in every location (for example, maple trees require long periods of cold weather to make the sap for maple syrup), yet all the ideas behind them can be widely applied. Some of the activities, such as boiling maple sap, work better with the supervision provided by parents, which is closer than that in a typical class. And often parents like a concrete result from their actions, so numerous activities satisfy that desire, such as the cozy stick houses. Children often are less concerned with making finished products than experimenting with, managing, rearranging, and playing with objects and environments, so activities are advised to those ends as well.

The book has a seasonal organization, but the standard four seasons don't have the same dates everywhere. Winter comes earlier and leaves later in northern parts of the Earth, and thus a gardening project in Maine has to be much more mindful of this short growing season than one in Arizona. Seasons are termed summer, autumn, winter, and spring, but families may learn other names related to their particular environment, such as "hurricane," "planting," or "fishing." And furthermore, as environmentalist in her book *The Sense of Wonder*, Rachel Carson noted, "There is something infinitely healing in the repeated refrains of nature—the assurance that dawn comes after night, and spring after winter." Young children sensitive to the routines of their individual lives can also tune in to, and find comfort in, nature's routines. In a graceful touch, Monica and Karen honor the primacy of the seasons with an original poem beginning each section.

The season poems along with many others, both original and well-known, exemplify a theme of this book: **many modes of expression and response to natural phenomena**. Painting, dancing, drawing, writing, building, making and using butterfly wings, fingerplays, singing, inventing, imitating, and caring for things are major observable responses. Sometimes children silently observe and later, sometimes much later, perhaps at bedtime, demonstrate what they have taken in. Notably, in this book, naming things is much less important than noticing, observing, and re-creating through multiple means. Young children are open to learning in many ways—their active minds range quickly over possibilities. If play with others—siblings, parents, friends—can be part of the response, so much the better. Play, with its fun and freedom, brings the concepts, vocabulary, social and motor skills, and other desirables along in its wake. And indeed, the lightness of the authors' prose underlines this.

A second theme of this book is **nature's abundance**. Layers of crispy bright leaves invite running, shuffling, flinging, collecting, sorting, and crafting. If a parent shakes a just-ready branch of blossoms over a child, the shower is delighting. Pinecones, fir cones, gleaming chestnuts, sprouting acorns, flying seeds from dandelions, milkweed, thistles. Brown cattail heads packed with seeds. Golden fields of mustard and dandelions. Bushes drooping with sweet berries. Stones, pebbles, gravel, broken shell bits, whole shells. So much

to touch, and finger, and smell, and pinch, and, if irresistible, stash in a pocket. So much to love, really. And different from inside, not needing to be put away. Everything is where it belongs already but can be played with. Snowflakes, raindrops, rainy creeks. Such things are close at hand, but take a look around—how many trees, hills, mountains? Look up, so many clouds changing all the time, in different shapes and sizes. On a clear night, note the abundance of stars, especially in a dark area. Truly there is plenty to go around, to share together, to rejoice in.

Much of the abundance shows visual beauty, even if transitory. Bright leaves turn dull brown, flowers wither, and snowflakes melt. The authors provide ways for children to savor and save beauty through art activities, such as leaf wreaths and sun catchers, and poems help children remember what they have experienced. Beauty is important in education because, as Rachel Carson also wrote, "Those who contemplate the beauty of the earth find reserves of strength that will endure as long as life lasts." When we help children notice beauty, their spirits are nourished.

This is a book to page through, looking for ideas that interest you. Monica and Karen invite you to "take a wander." Take a wonder too, because there is so much to this world we live in and noticing and cherishing can be a richly rewarding part of your lives.

CULTIVATING NATURE PLAY

Nature play can kindle a lasting love of nature and compassion for other living things. This book celebrates nature and the many playful ways we can explore outdoors with children.

WHAT IS NATURE PLAY?

Simply put, nature play is the freedom for children to explore and play in nature at their whim and in their own way, without adult interference. Children are empowered when they can freely choose how and what to do during nature play. This open-ended approach builds confidence and trust between child and adult. The sensory-rich encounters in nature are curious or strange sometimes, other times exhilarating and unexpected. The intensity of play, the creative scenarios children dream up, and the moments of quiet discovery are enriched by natural materials and settings that can never be replicated or fully experienced indoors.

Although the word *nature* may suggest that nature is a fixed place or a thing, nature is more aptly described as "us." People, like other animals, are an integral part of nature found in wild habitats and urban settings alike. Nature is not a place we must drive far away to visit; nature is everywhere, and we are a part of it. Time in nature, and specifically nature play, helps children reinforce this essential understanding about what it means to be alive, in and of the earth.

The word *play* as applied here describes the urges, instincts, and interests children naturally have when given the freedom to make their own choices. Play is the basis for exploring all kinds of learning across cognitive, social, emotional, physical, spiritual, and linguistic domains. Play is a universal child passion and, as many of us believe, a sacred right.

Play doesn't require instructions from adults or involve adult narration. Independence, curiosity, problem solving, creativity, resilience, and fun collide in a flurry of learning when children are at play. Children instinctively know how to play and have ideas about what they would like to explore or try to do in any given setting. This is true of play in cultures the world over.

Nature play, like nature, is much more than meets the eye. Nature play opens up a world of possibilities to connect with the land and its history, the complexities of the local ecosystem and its natural resources, the community, and others who explore and play together. Nature play stirs a remembrance inside us, a deep undeniable desire to connect with other living things, no matter how small. Leaf by leaf, children grow their own personal understanding about what it means to be part of nature. Compassion, empathy, kindness, and respect flourish as we live out the interconnectedness of this place we call home.

KEY BENEFITS OF NATURE PLAY

Play is obviously fun and interesting to kids, but some people don't realize the immense learning that happens through play. Our bodies and minds were designed to relate to nature for survival and nature play continues to manifest this basic human instinct. Further, studies show that nature play specifically enhances learning beyond indoor play experiences.

The benefits, listed to the right, multiply the more frequently children engage in nature play. This is not an exhaustive list, as the benefits of nature play are many! Given that the average child spends just 4 to 7 minutes outside, parents and educators alike can strive to provide greater access to nature play so children can benefit from the positive effects on their overall development.

> Fresh air
> Exposure to vitamin D from sunshine
> Exposure to naturally occurring bacteria, *Mycobacterium vaccae*, in soil
> Improved fine and gross motor development from active physical-play opportunities
> Understanding of healthy foods and nutritional needs (foraging and edible gardening)
> Healthy eye development
> Supported risk taking
> Improved cognition (high-order thinking and executive functioning skills)
> Space and time to observe, experiment, and problem solve
> Direct real-world links to curriculum
> Stress reduction and calming effects
> Opportunities to feel and express empathy, compassion, kindness, respect, and gratitude
> Appreciation for the land, its history, and indigenous cultures
> Self reflection and perspective taking
> Spirituality, a sense of belonging, and connectedness
> Opportunities to experience, process, and integrate sensory input
> Social and independent play that fosters determination, grit, perseverance, and self confidence
> Desire to act positively as caretakers who share the natural world and its resources

EMERGENT CURRICULUM AND INTENTIONAL EXPERIENCES

Often referred to as "emergent curriculum," children naturally stretch their skills as they experience the unpredictable (emergent) aspects of nature and respond based on their evolving interests and needs. Like nature play, emergent curriculum is not directed by adults. Rather, emergent curriculum may be facilitated, observed, and documented by adults who are keen to understand how child development naturally unfolds.

Nature play and emergent curriculum can dovetail with intentional approaches to school curriculum and more traditional forms of learning. For this reason, we have decided to share a balance of playful nature experiences that are paired with activities you and your child can enjoy together. The nature play experiences have varying degrees of adult interaction (from none to very little), while the projects are more directed and build upon your child's understanding of seasonal topics.

*"The child who has cared for another living thing …
is more easily led to care for his own life."*
—Friedrich Froebel

RISKS VERSUS HAZARDS: YES, THEY CAN CLIMB TREES!

Author and researcher Helen Tovey suggests that we should question if we want a culture of *protection* or *resilience* when it comes to raising our children. We must decide if the relative danger of climbing a tree is worth the mastery and confidence of perching atop.

To be sure, there are hazards that adults should be aware of and plan for. A hazard is something that can cause death or debilitating injury, and not something a child can readily judge on their own. Responsible adults, not children, must determine what hazards may be present in any given setting. Hazards vary depending on where you live but can include severe weather or wind, extreme temperatures, busy roads, falling branches or rocks, bodies of water, unfamiliar people, harmful plants (such as poison ivy), or potentially dangerous wildlife (ticks, spiders, bees, ants, venomous snakes, scorpions, wild cats, and so on). With preparation, adults can prevent and respond to hazardous situations, so they need not keep children from the benefits of nature play. (*Note: In addition to specialized training, safety routines and site assessments are an important part of any high-quality outdoor learning program.*)

But what about *risk* in outdoor play? Like climbing a tree or balancing on logs? There's a sweet spot of fun, excitement, and, yes, risk, that children can learn to assess for themselves.

Not so long ago, it was common for children to run barefoot outside or trek into the woods for playful adventures. As adults increasingly remove risks to make play "safe," children still seek out risky play. Some children go to extreme lengths to create their own exciting play opportunities on static or predictable playground settings, which can be far more dangerous than nature play. It is better to support children as they learn to calculate risk and make sensible decisions on their own, based on their interests and abilities.

The distinction between risk and hazard is crucial. Adults must be vigilant about hazards and responsible for monitoring or removing them. Risks, on the other hand, are beneficial for children. Children are capable of assessing many risks during outdoor play, but it requires a degree of trust from adults. Ultimately, the benefits of taking risks outweigh a scraped elbow or bruised shin, though you may wince or hold your breath at times! The idea of risk also transcends physicality, however, because taking an emotional risk (like talking to a new friend or sharing a special toy) is just as important. If we want children to become confident and resilient, then we should find ways to support risk taking during nature play.

Note: You know your child best. Supported risks should be appropriate for your child's age, experience, and abilities.

HOW CAN PARENTS AND CAREGIVERS ENCOURAGE MORE NATURE PLAY?

> Give time, space, and permission.

> Turn off, tune out, slow down.

> Provide frequent access to safe wild spaces (garden, park, yard, schoolyard, farm, nature center, or other natural habitats).

> Take action to green outdoor spaces.

> Get involved in the school parent-teacher organization. Advocate for nature play and schoolyard habitats.

> Plan for family time in nature. Put it on the calendar and plan on being outdoors together.

> Enjoy meal times outside.

> Go on outings with friends or another family, and schedule playdates or meet-ups.

> Join clubs, camps, or other extracurricular activities. They may not be entirely child directed, but they may provide opportunities for nature play.

> Wonder out loud. Set an example. Let your children see you enjoying time outdoors.

> Model eco-friendly habits and talk about why you live this way (native gardening, feeding the birds, recycling and composting, bringing your canteen, skipping the straw, bringing your own bag, picking up litter when in nature, donating used items instead of trashing them).

> Live by "leave no trace" principles.

WHAT DO I NEED FOR NATURE PLAY?

The truth of the matter is that if you have safe access to outdoor space, that's all you need. But like most things, when you plan ahead, the experience can be more meaningful.

BEFORE YOU PLAY

These tips will help you make the most of outdoor play:

> **Safety first.** Always keep your first-aid kit (along with life-saving medicine like an EpiPen) in your backpack. It can be helpful to have bug repellant, sunscreen, and lip balm too.

> **Gear up.** When children (and adults!) are dressed for the weather, nature play is more enjoyable. Base layers and waterproof gear are key for cold or wet weather.

> **Pack a snack.** Be sure to have fresh water in your canteen and a few snack items such as whole fruits, nuts, or granola.

Now that you're prepared with the basics, there are additional tools and materials that can extend nature play and enhance your child's skill development.

BACKPACK EXTRAS

> Binoculars
> Field guides
> Trail pails or recycled containers for collection
> Phone apps (eBird, iNaturalist)
> Bandana for games
> Nature journal or sketchbook
> Tools for writing, drawing, or painting
> Small empty jars/containers
> Scissors
> Tape
> Mallets
> Magnifier

There are plenty of other items you could bring outside, but this is a nice list for starters. Keep a backpack by the front door or in your trunk so you are always ready for nature play!

GET SCHOOLED: NATURE-BASED EDUCATION

Nature-based schools such as nature preschools, forest kindergartens, forest schools, and nature-based childcare centers are becoming more widespread. Many public schools incorporate weekly Forest Day programs to integrate outdoor learning as part of a holistic curriculum. Other schools obtain "green school" status as a demonstration of their commitment to Earth-friendly practices. Natural play spaces, schoolyard habitats, and garden initiatives are also a growing part of this movement.

THE FLOW OF THIS BOOK

This introduction highlights key benefits and approaches to nature play so you can get to it! Chapters 1 through 4 are organized broadly by season: summer, autumn, winter, and spring. Chapter 5 describes several ideas for year-round nature play.

We encourage you to flip through the guide and select nature play experiences and activities based on your child's interests. There is no prescribed sequence to follow because what you decide to do will vary based on the interests, ages, and abilities of children in your care. The time of year and places you choose to explore will also factor into how you use this book. Each chapter contains playful outdoor experiences and activities that span many topics and skills, all of which promote nature connection.

These four headings appear throughout the book:

❯ **Nature Play Experience**
❯ **Make It Wild**
❯ **Keep It Wild**
❯ **Extending the Experience**

Nature Play Experience invites you to interact with the natural world. Experiences may suggest approaches to observation, documentation, exploration, or reflection in a specific habitat or season. These include invitations to wander and play in an unstructured way, or they may suggest an activity with a more focused intention. While we always advocate for unstructured, child-directed play, nature play experiences may fluidly move between your child's interests and intentional opportunities you share to learn about an aspect of nature. It's important that parents provide ample space and time for children to play and explore. To this end, adults should use the nature play experiences based on interests that children have demonstrated. If your child loves rocks, start in chapter 5!

Make It Wild features a nature-based project or activity that builds upon the nature play experience. Natural materials are incorporated in recipes, experiments, art projects, and more to help scaffold learning about a concept or support further inquiry about a given topic.

Keep It Wild provides safety tips or reminders relevant to each nature play experience or project.

Extending the Experience offers a deeper way to explore a seasonal topic.

Chapter 6 provides a special glimpse into perspectives on outdoor learning and play from a wide variety of nature-based educators. Chapter 7 is full of templates so you can pull out a page and take it with you on an adventure. The resources and reference sections include further information about selected nature play and natural history topics. Of particular note are the selected children's books that correspond with each chapter.

We hope you enjoy sunny skies, mud pies, and all the seasonal adventures that await!

1

SEASONAL NATURE PLAY:
SUMMER

Nature revels in summer, dressed in leafy foliage and wild blankets of flowers. Animals search for mates, care for young, and forage for food. Birds and insects seem to celebrate as they sing. Warm breezes beckon us outside amid a colorful swirl of plants and animals making the most of sun-drenched days. Creatures are crawling under every frond and dancing over the treetops. Every habitat is buzzing with activity so it's an ideal season to get outdoors for nature play!

SUMMER COMES TO TOWN

by Karen Madigan

Birdsong wakes the sleepy morning with cheerful hum and chatter.
Gentle rain spills from clouds with quiet pitter-patter.
Mushrooms burst, mosses pop, ferns unfurl their fronds.
Dragonflies go whirring by as turtles laze in ponds.
Our shining star, the sun, appears and warms the earth and air.
Snails and slugs and salamanders leave their gloomy lairs.
Marigolds and violets dressed in lofty gowns, have gifts to share with everyone
as summer comes to town.

CHANGING SKY

NATURE PLAY EXPERIENCE

The sky's canvas comes in countless shades during summer, from light blue with big puffy clouds to pastel pinks and oranges at sunset. The intense dark grays of summer storms can quickly change to a cloudy purple haze or perhaps even a rainbow. The star of the show by far is the Sun! We owe our existence to its bright light and warmth. On a sunny morning, head outside and take a walk. Collect natural items to create a sundial.

MAKE IT WILD: SUNDIAL

Sundials were first used to tell time as early as 1500 BCE, and possibly even earlier. These instruments can be as simple as a stick poked into the ground or as elaborate as a hand-carved sculpture. A sundial consists of a disk or dial and a gnomon (stick or pole protruding from the center). A shadow is cast when the Sun shines on the gnomon. The shadow moves as the Sun rises or sets in the sky, indicating the hour of day. The hemisphere you live in will determine how you will make your sundial.

Note: You can make a sundial anywhere the Sun casts shadows with open space outside. It's best to start early in the morning so you have a chance to add a seashell or stone for each hour of the day.

MATERIALS

› **12 large seashells or stones**
› **Large stick or straight piece of driftwood**
› **Watch or timer**

PROCESS

1. Find a clear, flat area to make your sundial.
2. Place your stick (gnomon) vertically into the ground.
3. Mark where the shadow falls with one shell or stone and make note of the time on your watch.
4. Place the remaining shells in a circle around the gnomon, like a clock.
5. Check the sundial on the hour, every hour, until sundown.
6. Adjust the shells according to the shadow.

KEEP IT WILD

In the Northern Hemisphere, lean the gnomon to true north. If you are in the Southern Hemisphere, lean it to true south. Your smartphone likely has a compass that will show these directions.

 ## EXTENDING THE EXPERIENCE

A mandala is a geometric design consisting of repeated patterns that create a circle. In some Eastern religions, a mandala is a symbolic representation of the universe that is used for meditation. Use found treasures to make a nature mandala. Pinecones, shells, stones, sea glass, driftwood, leaves, grasses, and more can be used to create beautiful mandalas. You can do this anywhere with all sorts of natural loose parts. We will revisit this activity in the winter chapter.

FLOWERS

NATURE PLAY EXPERIENCE

As summer begins to wind down, flowers bow their heads and drop their seeds. Visit a garden in late summer to collect flowers that have wilted or are beginning to fade. Do the flowers have a scent? Children can pull the petals from the flower heads to examine the seeds inside. Sort flowers by size, color, or variety. Some flowers, such as marigolds or bee balm, can also be used to make natural dye.

MAKE IT WILD: MARIGOLD DYE

MATERIALS

> 4–6 cups (900–1350 ml) marigold flowers (dried or fresh with stems removed)
> Nonreactive dye pot (such as a stainless steel pot)
> Water
> Strainer
> Half a yard of cotton, muslin, or silk fabric
> Tongs

PROCESS

1. Place the marigold flower heads in the pot and cover them with water.

2. Heat on medium-high heat until simmering for at least 30 minutes, stirring occasionally.

3. Strain the dye into a bowl to remove flowers. Return the dye to the pot.

4. Wet your fabric under warm water and squeeze out excess water.

5. Place the fabric in the dye pot and simmer for 30 minutes.

6. Turn off the heat and let fabric sit in the dye pot for 1 hour.

7. Using tongs, remove the fabric from pot and let cool in a bowl.

8. Rinse the fabric to remove excess dye. Hang to dry.

KEEP IT WILD

Plant a dye garden! Calendula, coreopsis, hollyhock, bee balm, and marigolds can all be used for natural dyeing. Sow lots of seeds in spring for a mid- to late-summer harvest of flowers—and a nectar source for pollinators.

EXTENDING THE EXPERIENCE

Experiment with different amounts of mordant and marigold flowers for a variety of deep golden shades. To mordant the fabric, add 2 to 3 tablespoons (28 to 42 g) alum and 1 to 2 tablespoons (14 to 28 g) cream of tartar to half a gallon (2 l) of water in a bowl. Stir to dissolve, add the fabric to the bowl, and soak for 1 hour or longer before adding the fabric to the dye pot. Try painting with your dye in your nature journal or using it in some of the other projects in this book.

NOCTURNAL LIFE

NATURE PLAY EXPERIENCE

Nighttime in summer is a treat for the senses! Watching fireflies blink and listening to night sounds such as crickets, tree frogs, and other nocturnal creatures is fascinating. Enjoy the summer evening with a "sit spot" experience. Head outside, find a place to sit, and bring awareness to the sights and sounds around you. Meditation, breathing, or mindfulness techniques can intensify the experience. Don't use a flashlight! Like other animals, our eyes naturally adjust to the changing level of light as darkness falls.

MAKE IT WILD: INSECT OBSERVATION

MATERIALS

> White or light-colored bedsheet
> Clothesline or rope
> Black light, flashlight, or any other type of light
> Camera

PROCESS

1. Hang the sheet on a clothesline or rope tied between trees.

2. Set up a light (black light works best) to illuminate the sheet.

3. Observe and photograph the creatures that appear on the sheet.

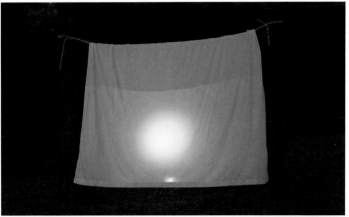

KEEP IT WILD

Moths are attracted to all types of artificial light, especially to ultraviolet light. Recent studies show how certain species of moths are evolving to avoid artificial light sources. This moth evolution could decrease pollination and food sources for nocturnal animals such as bats. Eek! Unless you need outdoor lights, please turn them off.

EXTENDING THE EXPERIENCE

Leave your sheet out overnight and check it the next day. Are there other creatures that were not present during your nighttime observation?

HUMMINGBIRDS

NATURE PLAY EXPERIENCE

Where there are flowers, you just may find hummingbirds humming about. Visit a habitat that hosts hummingbirds, such as a garden, meadow, or backyard. Explore the habitat and look closely at blossoms, grasses, and trees that grow there. What are the hummingbirds busy doing? Use binoculars to get a close-up view—if you can keep up! What do you notice about the way the tiny birds move? What do you wonder about hummingbirds? What plants and animals share this habitat with the hummingbirds? Spend several minutes observing with a still body and quiet voice to a catch of glimpse of these beautiful little birds.

MAKE IT WILD: HUMMINGBIRD NECTAR AND JAR FEEDER

Hummingbirds need a tremendous amount of energy to fuel their bodies. You can make some energizing hummingbird nectar that mimics the nectar the birds get from real flowers. Although most hardware and gardening stores sell hummingbird feeders, you can create your own adorable feeder from a few household items.

MATERIALS

> 1 cup (150 g) refined white sugar

> 4 cups (946 ml) warm water

> 12 inches (30 cm) ribbon, twine, or yarn

> Canning ring

> Scissors

> Mesh produce bag (any color)

> 1 (4-ounce [120 ml]) canning jar

PROCESS

1. Make the nectar by combining the sugar and water; mix until sugar dissolves and then set aside.
2. Tie ribbon onto either side of the canning ring to make a loop for hanging (as shown in photo).
3. Cut a 6-inch (15 cm) square from the mesh produce bag.
4. Place the mesh square over the mouth of the jar, then twist the ring on and trim the excess fabric. (Be careful not to cut the ribbon.)
5. Fill the jar with nectar, then hang it outside by the looped ribbon.
6. Watch for hummingbirds!

Note: It is not necessary to boil the nectar. Leftover nectar can be refrigerated for up to 3 weeks. Remember to change the nectar in your feeder every few days.

KEEP IT WILD

If you plant nectar sources, hummingbirds will surely visit your yard or porch. Ideal hummingbird flowers include cardinal flower (*Lobelia cardinalis*), bee balm (*Monarda didyma*), and native species of columbine, salvia, lupine, rhododendron, and lily.

 ## EXTENDING THE EXPERIENCE

When you notice hummingbirds visiting your feeder, spend some time observing them. How many are you able to notice? Track them with your eyes as they flit away from the feeder. Can you see where they go? Do they perch anywhere? Make notes about hummingbird visits in your nature journal or on your natural events calendar. You may begin to see a pattern, and if you continue to refill your jar, your speedy friends will return.

SPIDERS AND WEBS

NATURE PLAY EXPERIENCE

How lucky we are to observe the intricate weaving that spiders do. Spiderwebs are like priceless works of art hidden in nature. Sometimes it's tough to see the webs while hiking a trail. Slow down on your walk and look between trees or shrubs. Gently mist webs you see with a spray bottle. This will highlight the delicate traps so you can take in their splendor and complexity. You may even spy the artist herself wrapping up a meal. Draw the webs in your nature journal using white or light-colored pastels on dark paper

MAKE IT WILD: SPIDERWEB WEAVING PROVOCATION

A provocation is an open-ended suggestion for using materials. Providing the materials without any specific directions leaves it up to the artist to create whatever they wish.

MATERIALS
> **Sticks**
> **Scissors**
> **Yarn**

PROCESS
1. Gather materials after your spiderweb walk.
2. Sit near the edge of a forest or meadow.
3. Channel your inner spider and weave away!

KEEP IT WILD

Spiders are part of nature's delicate balance. Though some people are fearful of spiders, they are a food source for birds, frogs, chipmunks, turtles, and many other animals. Pesticides that kill spiders and insects can also harm the creatures that rely on them for food. Popular culture may sensationalize certain animals like spiders, sharks, snakes, or bats, which can cause alarm when children come upon them. Adults are crucial role models of positive, respectful attitudes for all living things. Help your child understand that it is okay (and natural!) to be nervous when encountering unfamiliar animals. But we can show respect for all creatures by doing them no harm and keeping our distance.

 EXTENDING THE EXPERIENCE

Read the following poem aloud, then try your hand at writing a poem, story, or song inspired by our arachnid friends.

SPIDER SPIDER

by Karen Madigan

Spider, spider craft your web,

Make it out of silken thread.

Spinnerets release thread to the breeze,

The air will take it to the trees.

Send it out, reel it in.

Repeat, repeat, repeat again.

Catch your prey in sticky string,

Eat your lunch and spin again!

BEES AND BUTTERFLIES

NATURE PLAY EXPERIENCE

Whether in a garden or just a small pot of posies, butterflies and bees will visit your flowers. Did you know that you can attract these important pollinators with a few pieces of fruit on a plate? Visit a botanical garden, butterfly sanctuary, or community garden plot to get up close and personal with these beautiful creatures. Take along your nature journal and spend some time sitting among the flowers. Once you've had time to observe the insects fluttering about, think about traits that bees and butterflies share. How do bees move compared to butterflies? How many species of bees and butterflies can you count? What color flowers do they seem to be most attracted to? How are their wings different?

MAKE IT WILD: WATERCOLOR BUTTERFLY CAPE

MATERIALS

> White bedsheet or fabric (cotton, muslin, or silk)
> Pencil or light-colored marker
> Scissors
> Jars
> 1 cup (250 ml) water
> ½ cup (125 ml) fabric medium (will allow watercolors to become permanent on fabric)
> Ribbon
> Hole punch
> Liquid watercolors/ natural dyes in various colors
> Water
> Paintbrushes

PROCESS

1. Fold the bedsheet in half and draw a wing shape away from the folded edge.

2. Keeping sheet folded, cut along the line to make wings.

3. Fill a jar with 1 cup (250 ml) water.

4. Add ½ cup (125 ml) of fabric medium to the water and mix. Set aside.

5. Add liquid watercolors and/or natural dyes to jars. Add a little fresh water to each color and stir.

6. Paint the wings with watercolors as desired, symmetrically or any way you like.

7. Paint over the wings with the fabric medium/water mixture.

8. Allow the wings to air dry, then toss in the clothing dryer on high heat for 10 minutes to set.

9. Cut or punch holes at the base of the wings, slip a ribbon through, and tie the wings on.

10. Wear your wings and fly!

KEEP IT WILD

Many insects are pollinators. Bees, flies, beetles, and butterflies all help flowers and trees make seeds by spreading pollen from blossom to blossom. Other creatures like bats and hummingbirds help pollinate too. Help these busy critters by creating a pollinator garden with flowers such as purple coneflower, giant sunflowers, milkweed, New York ironweed, aster, bee balm, and goldenrod. Herbs such as mint, lavender, parsley, and sage are also excellent sources of nectar and pollen. Joe-Pye weed is an outstanding plant and will attract more butterflies than you can imagine! Please "bee kind" and never use poisonous weed or bug killers in your garden. Find experts in your community for advice on the best pollinator plants for your area.

 EXTENDING THE EXPERIENCE

Honey comes in many varieties depending on the nectar source. Orange blossom, wildflower, clover, and blueberry are a few kinds of honey flavors. Look for honey harvest festivals in your area or visit an apiary to taste the sweet honey of the bees.

BEE AND FLOWER FINGERPLAY

by Karen Madigan

The bee loves the flower.

The flower loves the bee.

They are good friends as you can see.

"I have nectar" says the flower,

"I have pollen" says the bee,

"Thank you" says the flower,

"Buzz!" says the bee.

Note: You can use American Sign Language to act out this fingerplay.

FORAGING

NATURE PLAY EXPERIENCE

Berries are at their prime in summer. Ripe and ready for picking, berries are useful, nutritious, and delicious! Whether you have a garden that includes them or you set out to find some growing wild in a forest or meadow, whole berries are a sweet addition to any meal or the magic ingredient in a wide variety of recipes. Go on a wander in search of edible, ripe berries. Did the birds eat all of your berries? Visit a local farm that offers berry picking and load up!

MAKE IT WILD: MIXED BERRY SUN TEA

MATERIALS

> ½ cup (50 g) foraged and washed herbal plants and flowers (chamomile, mint, spicebush, sassafras, lemon balm, raspberry leaves, calendula, or elderflower)

> Quart-size (950 ml) jar or container with lid

> Water

> Sunshine

> ½ cup (75 g) washed mixed berries (raspberries, blackberries, strawberries, elderberries, or blueberries)

PROCESS

1. Place the washed herbs in the jar and fill with water.
2. Place the jar in a sunny spot and leave for at least 4 hours.
3. Add the berries and let sit for 30 minutes to 1 hour (or longer).
4. Strain the tea into ice-filled glasses, add a few berries, and enjoy!

Note: You can also try additions such as lemon or orange peel, cloves, honey, agave nectar, or candied ginger.

KEEP IT WILD

Forage safely! Do not eat any herbs or flowers you cannot identify. Forage with permission, take only what you will use, and do not harvest rare or protected plants.

EXTENDING THE EXPERIENCE

Many berries can make vibrant natural dye, including blueberries, raspberries, and cherries. Simmer 1 part fruit to 4 parts water until you reach your desired color, about 30 minutes. Once it cools, paint with the berry dye in your nature journal or experiment with dyes on pre-fixed natural fabric like muslin or silk.

SHELTER

NATURE PLAY EXPERIENCE

During the hot summer days, it's wonderful to find a shady place to play or just relax in nature. Some trees and shrubs offer lofty, leafy branches that droop down for a no fuss hideout. Other trees or bushes may grow closely together and naturally define a cozy space. Spend time in a hidden-away spot. Perhaps a tea party, small-worlds play, or pretend camping will be part of today's nature play.

Note: Learn more about small-worlds play in chapter 5.

MAKE IT WILD: POLE BEAN VINE SHELTER

Pole beans are easy to grow and will climb high in just a few weeks! There are many varieties, such as Scarlet Runner, Purple Podded, Blue Lake, and Kentucky Wonder. Plant more than one variety if you wish.

MATERIALS

> 8 (6-foot [1.8-m]) bamboo poles
> Twine
> Pole bean seeds (any variety)
> Organic soil
> Water

PROCESS

1. Choose a sunny location and prepare it for planting.
2. Poke the bamboo poles into the ground to form a semicircle.
3. Gather the tops of the poles together and secure with twine.
4. Plant three bean seeds (1 inch [2.5 cm] deep and 2 inches [5 cm] apart) around each pole.
5. Water regularly and watch your beans grow.
6. Enjoy your shelter and delicious bean harvest!

KEEP IT WILD

Enhance your soil with compost to increase the chances of healthy bean plants. You can add a layer of mulch around your plantings to keep moisture in and provide a cushiony place to sit under your shelter.

EXTENDING THE EXPERIENCE

Experiment with other types of climbing vines, such as black-eyed Susan, squash, or mini pumpkins for your next shelter.

SEASONAL NATURE PLAY:
AUTUMN

Fading light, colorful leaves, and crisp air signal the arrival of fall. The autumnal equinox means less daylight as darkness falls sooner than in summer. Plants and animals are keen to prepare for colder weather now that a chill is in the air. With cozy scarves and warm mugs of tea, we are ready for another beautiful season of nature play.

FRUITS IN FALL
by Monica Wiedel-Lubinski

Pears and apples on the trees,
Hanging low in autumn's breeze.
Squash and pumpkins on the vine,
Pick them now, they're ripe and fine.
Harvest, gather, taste them all,
We give thanks for fruits in fall.

CHANGING SKY

NATURE PLAY EXPERIENCE

Venture outdoors as daylight dwindles and twilight sets in. Notice insect calls and the movement of bustling birds as they settle into evening darkness. Where do crickets and spiders go at night? What are squirrels and chipmunks doing? Which birds seem most active now? What other animals might be waking up as night falls? Look for clues that help tell the story of these animals at dusk.

MAKE IT WILD: LEAF LANTERNS

Evening holds a magic all its own in autumn. Use colorful leaves from the season to create a glowing lantern.

MATERIALS

> Assorted pressed leaves
> Grapevine, bittersweet, or wisteria vine clippings
> Tacky craft glue
> Shallow dish for glue (like a clean lid or yogurt container)
> Flat brush to spread glue
> Clean jam, pasta sauce, or canning jar (the bigger, the better)
> Scraps of white or light-colored gift tissue paper
> Cotton or hemp twine
> Battery-operated tea light

PROCESS

1. Gather an assortment of colorful leaves during nature play.

2. Press the leaves between heavy book pages for at least 1 week.

3. Once leaves are pressed, gather vine clippings so they are fresh for use. (If you gather vines ahead of time, soak them in warm water to ensure they are soft and pliable.)

4. Squeeze some tacky glue into a shallow dish and use a brush to cover the jar with the glue.

5. Press and smooth tissue paper and leaves onto the glue-covered jar.

6. Use a thin layer of glue to cover and seal all of the leaves on the lantern. Set it aside to dry.

7. Add twine and vines to embellish the top of the lantern.

8. Turn on the tea light, place it in the lantern, and enjoy the glow!

Note: Remember to clean your brush and glue dish to use them again.

KEEP IT WILD

Leaf lanterns are enchanting luminaries, but if you want to turn on your own night vision, don't use artificial light at all. Let your eyes gradually adjust as dusk becomes night, and let your wild instincts kick in.

EXTENDING THE EXPERIENCE

Many cultures have seasonal celebrations of light. Consider starting an autumn solstice tradition with your family, neighborhood, or school.

SEEDS

NATURE PLAY EXPERIENCE

Seeds roll, float, fly, or hitch a ride to find fertile ground, and they are literally bursting to find homes in autumn. Explore a park or yard to gather and examine fall seeds. What seeds can you find? Remember, nuts like acorns are seeds and fall fruits cleverly conceal seeds too! How many different kinds of seeds can you find? Notice the variety of types, colors, and sizes in your area. What can we learn about where a seed grows based on its shape?

MAKE IT WILD: SEED SPIRAL

Most of us can appreciate the aesthetic beauty of the natural world. Artists like Andy Goldsworthy exemplify using nature to make temporary outdoor works of art.

PROCESS

1. Locate a clearing or glen to create the seed spiral. If you'd like to use it for a walking meditation, be sure to leave at least 3 feet (1 m) of space between the lines of the spiral for walking.

2. Gather a variety of seeds, fallen branches, and leaves.

3. Place seeds and other natural objects on the ground to make a large spiral.

4. Walk the spiral and invite others to experience your creation.

Your seed spiral will change over time as the weather, animals, and other forces of nature interact with it. Some seeds may even sprout in the spring! Visit your spiral often to see how it evolves. You can keep adding natural materials to it each time you visit or let nature take its course.

KEEP IT WILD

Many animals make food caches to prepare for winter. Leave plenty of seeds for the animals and expect that some will go missing from your seed spiral!

 ## EXTENDING THE EXPERIENCE

Experiment with the seeds to see what will grow. Plant some of these seeds now or let them harden in the freezer (which simulates winter) and save them for planting in the spring. Use your nature journal to record the date you planted the seeds. Make predictions about when they may sprout and what the seeds may grow into.

LEAVES

NATURE PLAY EXPERIENCE

Trek a leafy trail. Breathe in the scent of fall leaves. Feast your eyes on the colorful blanket of leaves above, below, and gently adrift in the sky. What colors dominate the tree silhouettes? Can you detect movement from animals hidden among fall foliage? As you play, gather favorite fall leaves to use in your leaf crown.

MAKE IT WILD: LEAF CROWNS

Become king or queen of the forest with these sweet autumn crowns.

MATERIALS

> Assorted leaves and grasses
> Clean pizza box lid
> Adult scissors
> Large embroidery needle
> Hemp twine or embroidery floss

PROCESS

1. Gather a basket full of colorful leaves and grasses.

2. Cut the pizza box lid into strips 2 inches (5 cm) wide by 20 inches (50 cm) long. (You may need an adult to help you cut through the thick cardboard.)

3. Test the sizing around your head with one of the strips.

4. Thread the needle with a piece of embroidery floss about the length of your arm and knot it at the end.

5. Arrange the first leaf onto the crown and stitch it into place. Continue adding leaves and stitches until the leaf crown is finished.

6. Stitch the ends of the cardboard to tie off the crown to wear it.

Note: Before you begin sewing, trying to poke the needle through the cardboard to see how hard you need to push. It helps to wiggle the needle in place and then push it through.

KEEP IT WILD

If you come upon millipedes, pill bugs, caterpillars, worms, or other tiny creatures on your leaf search, gently replace them just as you found them. Remember, we share nature with all living things.

 ## EXTENDING THE EXPERIENCE

Here are a few more ideas for leaf exploration:

- Grab an old pillowcase and fill it with leaves to make a leafy sit-upon.
- Try to match leaf colors with watercolor paints, then paint the backs of the leaves to make prints in your nature journal.
- See how many leaf shapes you can find (oval, star, heart, and so on), then try to identify the trees they are from.

FROST

NATURE PLAY EXPERIENCE

Legend has it that Jack Frost flies before dawn to conjure up sparkling frost over the land when cold autumn nights turn to day. Bundle up one early morn to see for yourself! Where do you notice the most frost? Are there any nooks where no frost formed? Notice how the leaves glisten like glass. Take a deep breath and savor a moment of gratitude for the beauty of the season. When you exhale, can you see the warm vapor of your breath hanging in the cold air? Make a prediction: how long will the frost stay today?

MAKE IT WILD: JACK FROST GLAZE

This salt solution mimics the crystal structures that form when dew turns to icy frost.

MATERIALS

> 2 cups (500 ml) water
> Pot
> 1 ¼ cups (300 g) Epsom salt
> 3–4 drops liquid dish soap
> Paintbrush
> Watercolor tray
> Sturdy watercolor paper or nature journal

PROCESS

1. Bring water to a boil in the pot.

2. Add the Epsom salt and stir until fully dissolved. Set aside to cool to warm.

3. When the salt water is warm (not boiling hot), add the drops of dish soap.

4. Dip the paintbrush first in the saltwater solution and then in the watercolor paint of your choice, then paint onto paper.

5. Once dry, you'll see how the salt crystal "frost" forms when water evaporates.

Note: Jack Frost glaze can be mixed with watercolor paint, food coloring, or ink. It can even be brushed onto a window pane or u bouquet of fall leaves to create a frosty effect. Be patient! You won't see the frosty effect until glaze is completely dry.

KEEP IT WILD

It's helpful to bundle up in waterproof mittens instead of fleece or knit ones. That way you can enjoy cold weather play without wet hands.

 ## EXTENDING THE EXPERIENCE

If frost is on the ground, it's an ideal time for a morning fire! Sip tea or enjoy a warm bowl of oatmeal fireside.

BIRDS

NATURE PLAY EXPERIENCE

Observe birds in autumn as they prepare for the colder weather to come. Do you notice the birds changing their tunes? Look around to detect changes in food for the birds. (Do you hear as many insects? Or notice plentiful berries?) If falling leaves have changed colors, does the array of hues help birds search for food? How do autumn colors help birds protect themselves? How can you help make sure the birds and other animals have the food they need? Gather some treasures such as pinecones or magnolia seedpods to make a beautiful and healthy treat for your animal friends.

MAKE IT WILD: PINECONE AND MAGNOLIA POD BIRD FEEDER

Use plentiful seedpods from nearby pine trees or magnolias to make a mobile that the birds are sure to love.

MATERIALS

> Seedpods

> Sturdy branch or stick

> Twine or ribbon

> Vegetable shortening, enough to spread evenly on your seedpods

> Spoon or butter knife for spreading shortening

> Birdseed in wide bowl

> Scissors

PROCESS

1. Gather seedpods and a sturdy stick during nature play.

2. Tie a length of twine or ribbon around each seed pod (about 6 to 12 inches [15 to 30 cm] long), then tie each seedpod onto your stick.

3. Spread the vegetable shortening on each seedpod.

4. Roll the seedpods in birdseed. Cover with as much seed as you can!

5. By now your hands are probably slippery, so wash them off if you need to.

6. Add a final piece of ribbon or twine at each end of the stick for hanging, then place the feeder somewhere you can watch the birds enjoy it.

KEEP IT WILD

When nature sheds leaves, many critters take shelter under them. Rake up a big pile of leaves that can remain in your yard, and you'll make another kind of bird feeder while you're at it! Likewise, when you put the garden to bed in autumn, leave the bare flowerheads for the birds to pluck.

 ## EXTENDING THE EXPERIENCE

For a fun take on suet cakes for your bird-feeding station, mix melted vegetable shortening with birdseed and dried fruits, then pour the mixture into paper-lined muffin tins. Lay a piece of ribbon in each "birdseed muffin" and cool in the fridge.

HARVEST

NATURE PLAY EXPERIENCE

Many plants and trees bear fruit during autumn's harvest. Go on a fruit search! What berries and fruits can you spy? Search in meadow grasses or along forest edges in the shrubs. Instead of picking these fruits, leave them for native animals to enjoy. Take photographs of the fruits you find and try to identify which plants produced them. You may be surprised to discover the bounty of berries at this time of year.

MAKE IT WILD: PUMPKIN APPLE SOUP

If you can visit a local pumpkin patch or apple orchard, now is the time to do it! Harvest these ingredients for a satisfying autumn soup.

MATERIALS

- 1 sugar or pie pumpkin
- Olive oil
- 3 apples (peeled, cored, and diced into cubes)
- 1 cup (160 g) chopped onion
- 1–2 garlic cloves to taste, finely chopped
- 3 tablespoons (45 g) butter
- 2–3 tablespoons (30–45 ml) honey or brown sugar
- ¼ teaspoon ground nutmeg
- ¼ teaspoon cinnamon
- 3 cups (720 ml) vegetable broth
- ½ cup (120 ml) heavy whipping cream
- ½ cup (120 ml) fresh apple cider
- Roasted pumpkin seeds for garnish

PROCESS

1. Preheat the oven to 350°F (180°C or gas mark 4).

2. Remove the pumpkin stem and seeds and slice the pumpkin into wedges. Drizzle with olive oil and place on parchment-lined baking sheet.

3. Roast the pumpkin until tender, about 40 to 50 minutes. Meanwhile, steam the apples until tender, about 10 minutes, then let cool.

4. Scoop the pumpkin flesh into a bowl. It will separate nicely from the skin when tender. Puree the cooked pumpkin and apple, then set aside.

5. Lightly sauté the chopped onions and garlic in butter on low heat until soft and golden brown.

6. Mix the pumpkin, apple, garlic, onion, honey, nutmeg and cinnamon in a bowl; puree again.

7. Warm the vegetable broth on low in a saucepan.

8. Add the puree to the broth, followed by the heavy whipping cream and cider. Stir slowly until combined. Add salt and/or more honey to taste.

9. Puree with an immersion hand blender or food processor for a creamy texture.

10. Serve warm with roasted pumpkin seeds on top.

KEEP IT WILD

Some berries are harmful if ingested. Young children can become adept at berry identification, but no child should eat wild berries without permission.

EXTENDING THE EXPERIENCE

Compost the kitchen scraps from your recipe. Pumpkin stems, apple peels, and onion skins are perfect for compost pile and a great way to enrich your garden soil.

RETURNING TO SOIL

NATURE PLAY EXPERIENCE

Explore a wild space to observe autumn flowers, grasses, shrubs, and trees. Which plants and plant parts have faded or fallen to the ground? How will these natural objects return to the soil? Do you think they will decompose or sprout next spring?

Scout the area for rotting logs and examine them closely. How does the bark feel? Rough and sturdy? Spongy and soft? What is growing on or near the log? Choose a log and gently roll it away from you as if you are opening the front door to a hidden home. Watch quietly for a few moments to observe movement under the log. What can you spy under this log? When you are finished, gently roll the log back into place to "close the door" and respect this habitat.

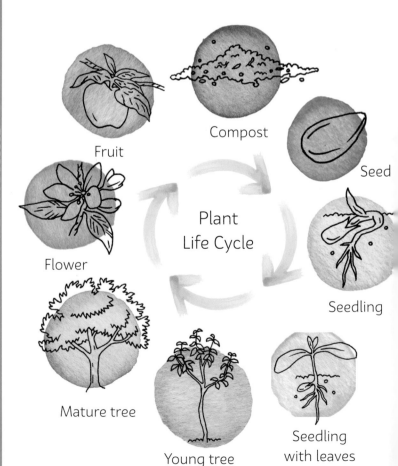

Fruit

Compost

Seed

Flower

Plant Life Cycle

Seedling

Mature tree

Young tree

Seedling with leaves

MAKE IT WILD: WILL IT ROT?

Conduct a simple experiment to discover how long these items will take to return to the soil.

MATERIALS

> Natural items such as evergreen needles, leaves, flowerheads, rocks, grass cuttings, fruit peels, or twigs

> Manufactured items such as a plastic bag, wrapper, or empty juice box, and cardboard box

> Container filled with soil

> Hand trowel (optional)

PROCESS

1. Gather your materials to use in the experiment.

2. Determine the length of the experiment, the longer the better (6 months, for example).

3. Make and record your predictions about which materials will decompose first.

4. Bury assorted natural and human-made materials in the container of soil.

5. Note where you bury each material along with your predictions.

6. Leave the container exposed to the weather for the designated period of days, weeks, or months.

7. Check on the materials at intervals (for example, once per month for 6 months) and photograph how they change.

8. When the experiment is done, compare the decomposition of materials to see if your prediction was correct. What broke down the fastest? Slowest? Did anything disappear?

KEEP IT WILD

Vermicompost and other compost piles are a great way to let nature decompose our food waste. Instead of sending it out with the trash headed to a landfill, compost at home to make nutrient-rich soil for the garden.

EXTENDING THE EXPERIENCE

Plants experience growing cycles of life and death as they move through the seasons. Many plants wither and die after fruiting. The process of decomposition breaks down leaves, seedpods, and stems and gradually returns them back into the soil. These enriching nutrients help new plants grow.

FORAGING

NATURE PLAY EXPERIENCE

There is still time to gather plants before they fade! Grab your favorite basket and go on a wander to look for common wood sorrel (*Oxalis acetosella*) and spearmint (*Mentha spicata*). There are many species of mint commonly found in herb gardens, such as peppermint or lemon balm, that make delicious tea.

Note: Avoid foraging along roadsides and other areas that may be treated with herbicides and pesticides.

MAKE IT WILD: SORREL AND MINT TEA

This is a refreshing tea that is easy to forage and tastes great warm or cold!

MATERIALS

> 1½ cups (375 ml) water

> 2 tablespoons (12 g) fresh wood sorrel

> 2 tablespoons (12 g fresh, 3 g dried) fresh or dried mint leaves

> Cheesecloth or sieve (a drawstring cheesecloth bag works well)

> Fresh squeezed lemon juice (optional)

> Honey to taste (optional)

PROCESS

1. Boil the water in a tea kettle.
2. Place the fresh wood sorrel and mint leaves into a pot.
3. Pour the boiling water over leaves and let sit for 5 minutes.
4. Strain the tea leaves using cheesecloth or a sieve.
5. Add a fresh squeeze of lemon juice or a dollop of honey to taste and stir well.
6. Enjoy your refreshing tea!

KEEP IT WILD

Have bunches of fresh spearmint? Freeze it in ice cubes for a cold, refreshing glass of water or mint-flavored iced tea. Fresh mint can also be used in berry smoothies, couscous and quinoa dishes, lime-seasoned snap peas, or watermelon and feta salad. It's a great introduction to many healthy recipes for your family to try when you forage this sweet, minty herb and cook together.

EXTENDING THE EXPERIENCE

Spicebush (*Lindera benzoin*) is plentiful in the understory of many North American forests. You can forage and dry the bright red berries and, when crushed, use them in place of allspice. Some call it "Appalachian Allspice" because of the bright, versatile flavor. Take time to discover how indigenous people where you live use spicebush—and countless other plants—for a variety of medicinal and dietary purposes.

ROOSTS AND DENS

NATURE PLAY EXPERIENCE

Take a wander in the woods to gather branches and sticks; they're especially easy to find after a windy fall day. This simple task often leads to the discovery of tiny creatures, plants, or fungi that make use of fallen branches. What lives on or beneath sticks? Is there a den hidden beneath a roof of fallen branches? Are there roosting nooks in hollow tree branches or abandoned nests? Sticks provide shelter and microhabitat for many creatures. Observe how this plentiful material supports wildlife around you in autumn. As you wander exploring sticks, scout out trees and sturdy shrubs you can lean branches on.

MAKE IT WILD: STICK FORT

Use baskets to hold small gathered twigs and make piles of larger branches. An assortment of sizes may be useful, depending on the size of your fort. Remember to use freshly fallen sticks from the trees. Bypass branches that are already decaying and inhabited by small animals. If you opt to build your fort near a bird feeder, you can quietly hunker down hidden from view and watch the birds.

MATERIALS

> Various size branches
> Leaves, grasses, or vines for outer covering (optional)
> Twine or nylon cord (optional)

PROCESS

1. Locate an ideal spot for your fort. (The crook of a tree 3 to 4 feet [1 to 1.2 m] from the ground makes a good starting point.)

2. Lean a long branch in the crook of the tree to create a central branch to lean others on.

3. Place branches perpendicular to the central branch to create walls.

4. Once the walls are in place, add leaves or bundles of grass to camouflage the fort.

5. When the fort is in place, you can add windows, a door, or other embellishments.

KEEP IT WILD

As you gather sticks for the fort, let rotting branches lie. They provide important food and shelter for small animals. Besides, they will likely fall apart if you try to use them for construction. As with all collecting, take only what you need, and use everything you take.

EXTENDING THE EXPERIENCE

Experiment with ways to create an original freeform fort. This is an engineering exercise of balanced design that will take patience and time, and it is far more fun with friends! While there are elaborate debris huts and shelters that are substantial enough for people to survive extreme cold, yours need not be fussy. Enjoy creating a cozy fort that feels just right for your nature play.

Note: Learn about the indigenous keepers of the land you frequent as a form of respect and to acknowledge past and present ways of knowing and being on the land. Teepees, wickiups, longhouses, and adobe houses are just a few examples of shelters indigenous people created in various parts of the world.

3

SEASONAL NATURE PLAY:
WINTER

There is much to see in winter that can be difficult to detect during the other seasons. The contour of the landscape is easier to observe when trees are bare. Winter woods seem to stretch far beyond what had been there just a few short weeks before. In cold climates, the experience of being in snow is magical. Winter is also a perfect time to look for animal clues such as tracks, fur, or bones.

Depending on where you live, winter may bring cold and snowy weather, or it could simply bring cooler-than-average temperatures. Spending time outside will offer opportunities to breathe fresh air, help your family build a healthy immune system, and provide much-needed activity and movement The proper gear makes all the difference for braving cold temperatures.

WINTER DAYS
by Monica Wiedel-Lubinski
Bare trees slumber,
As winter sets in.
Cold winds whirl,
Hibernation begins.
Shadows grow tall,
In the fading light of day
But when snowflakes fall,
We head outside to play!

CHANGING SKY

NATURE PLAY EXPERIENCE

From white and fluffy cumulus clouds to wispy streaks of cirrus, there are many clouds that appear in different seasons and temperatures. Clouds are made of water droplets, ice crystals, or both, that are suspended in the air. Some clouds hover high above the horizon, while others form at lower places in the sky. Clouds are good predictors of the weather. In winter, cirrostratus clouds are the most common. They are thin and will sometimes form a halo around the Sun.

On a day when cumulus clouds are high in the sky, grab a tarp or quilt and do some cloud watching. Are the clouds moving swiftly in the breeze? Are they changing and beginning to look like familiar shapes? What shapes do you see? Do the big puffy clouds look like pillows?

MAKE IT WILD: PINE NEEDLE AND LAVENDER CLOUD PILLOW

You can use this darling little pillow to cuddle with or slip it in a drawer to keep clothes smelling sweet.

MATERIALS

〉 Recycled denim or other fabric
〉 Scissors
〉 Sharp embroidery needle
〉 Embroidery floss
〉 Dried pine or balsam needles
〉 Dried lavender

PROCESS

1. Draw a cloud shape on the fabric.
2. Double the fabric and cut along the line.
3. Thread the needle and sew the pieces together along the edge, leaving a 1- to 2-inch (2.5 to 5 cm) opening.
4. Stuff the opening with pine needles and lavender.
5. Sew the pillow closed.

KEEP IT WILD

Grow lavender in your garden in the summer. Harvest the blossoms, dry them, and enjoy the sweet, earthy smell. Lavender has calming properties and can contribute to better sleep, so keep it close during a peaceful winter nap.

 ## EXTENDING THE EXPERIENCE

Use your new cloud pillow to lie back and watch the sky, then dip pine branches into homemade paint (see the recipe on page 84) and create cloudscapes in your nature journal.

TREES

NATURE PLAY EXPERIENCE

In winter it can be difficult to identify bare trees. With the exception of evergreen conifers, most deciduous trees are missing their biggest clues, their leaves! Armed with field guides, head outdoors with your family to a stand of unfamiliar trees. Each family member can choose a tree to explore. Are there any leaves still on the tree? Is the bark smooth or rough? Are twigs on the tree branches growing opposite or alternate? What clues, such as seeds, are on the ground nearby? Work together to identify your trees.

MAKE IT WILD: WINTER TREE SKETCHES

Observe and draw silhouettes of winter trees in your nature journal. If you've made any campfires, you can draw with a piece of cooled charcoal left behind.

MATERIALS

> Large tarp or quilt
> Nature journal
> Pencils, pastels, or charcoal

PROCESS

1. Spread out the tarp or quilt on the ground underneath some trees.

2. Lie on your back and look up at the trees for at least 10 minutes. Breathe deeply and observe the canopy without distraction.

3. Draw your observations in your nature journal.

4. If leaves or seedpods are nearby, you may want to sketch them. The shape and edges of the leaves can help reveal the identity of your trees.

KEEP IT WILD

Many field guides can help you hone plant and animal identification skills (see Resources on page 40). Although not useful for learning the process of identification, many apps can provide quick suggestions to help you identify a tree (iNaturalist is one example).

EXTENDING THE EXPERIENCE

You can place a page of your journal on top of tree bark and use pastels to make rubbings. Don't forget to hug your trees!

STARS

NATURE PLAY EXPERIENCE

Cold temperatures usually mean drier weather and more visibility for stargazing. Bundle up with your family on a clear winter night and head outside, preferably to an open area away from buildings and artificial light. It's best not to bring a flashlight with you, but you might want a thermos of hot cocoa! Some constellations are easy to spot with the naked eye, such as Orion's Belt. To help you focus, create the Star-Viewing Wand here. Snuggle up next to your loved ones and gaze at the stars!

MAKE IT WILD: STAR—VIEWING WAND

This sweet wand will inspire you to stargaze on a clear winter's night. Afterwards, you can use it for dramatic play.

MATERIALS

⟩ **5 sticks, each about 6 inches (15 cm) long**
⟩ **Raffia or yarn**
⟩ **Sturdy stick, about 12–16 inches (30–40 cm) long**
⟩ **Hot glue and glue gun (optional)**

PROCESS

1. Crisscross the sticks to form a star shape.
2. Use raffia or yarn to lash the star points together (hot glue is optional here).
3. Join the star to the larger stick by tying it on with raffia or yarn (hot glue optional).
4. Use your wand to peek at the night sky through the center of the star.

KEEP IT WILD

Try using a telescope to observe the night sky or create your own planetarium experience with a phone app like Star Rover, GoSkyWatch Planetarium, or Brittanica Kids: Solar System.

 ## EXTENDING THE EXPERIENCE

Embellish your Star-Viewing Wand with shimmery paint and ribbon! Keep track of the winter moon phases in your Moon journal (see page 135).

SNOW

NATURE PLAY EXPERIENCE

Bundle up for a winter walk and head out to a snowy forest. Use a basket or canvas bag to collect nature treasures such as sticks, evergreen branches, berries, nuts, and seeds. Spend some time sorting the objects and creating patterns.

No snow? No problem! You can create a nature mandala wherever you are.

MAKE IT WILD: SNOWY NATURE MANDALA

Making a nature mandala is a quiet and peaceful activity that allows your body and mind to slow down and be in the moment. This process of mindfulness lets you connect with each object as you place it in your design. There is no right or wrong way to create a mandala. It is a personal process and can be as simple or as elaborate as you choose.

MATERIALS

⟩ **Collected natural objects**

PROCESS

1. Place objects in a large circle. Sit in the center of the circle and close your eyes. Think about when you were collecting each object and where you found it. How did the object come to be where it was? Did it fall from a tree? Did an animal leave it there? Was it blown by the wind? Open your eyes and look around the circle at your items. Start by picking up the largest items. Look at each one closely. Is there anything you didn't notice before? How does it feel in your hands? Say the name of the item out loud. Begin to place the items in a pleasing design. Repeat with the remaining items until you decide that your mandala is complete. Spend some time looking at your work.

Note: This would be a great time to introduce meditation and sit spots as part of your nature awareness routines.

KEEP IT WILD

For some people, a daily practice of making mandalas is a relaxing form of meditation. Try it for a week to engage your senses and develop deeper appreciation for the abundance and beauty found in nature.

 ## EXTENDING THE EXPERIENCE

Make a snowy track mandala using your footsteps to create the design. No materials necessary, just yourself! Walk in a circle and then create various tracks and patterns. Drag your feet to make lines and jump or hop over the areas you wish to leave blank.

TRACKS

NATURE PLAY EXPERIENCE

Spend some searching for, following, and identifying animal tracks. Try to determine what the animals were up to and where they were going. Are there any other clues around, such as nut shells or scat? Do the tracks lead to a tucked-away den, or perhaps to a tree? Is there more than one type of tracks?

MAKE IT WILD: FOX AND GEESE

Fox walking is a way to move slowly, as if stalking prey silently like a fox would. To do it, hunch your head and shoulders forward, with your hands at your sides. Move slowly with fluid movements. Place one foot directly in front of the other in a straight line. With each step, place your heel down first, beginning with the outer edge of the foot. Roll slowly to the inner ball of the foot as you gently drop your toes. Fox walking helps heighten the awareness of our own bodies, improves our ability to control movements, and helps us go undetected like a stealthy predator. Fox walking is a skill often used in tracking animals. If there is no snow, you can draw a circular path on a sidewalk or blacktop with chalk.

CREATE THE TRACK

1. Walk in a circle to create a large path with your footprints.

2. Bisect the circle by shuffling across it from one side to the other until the tracks make an X in the center of the circle.

3. Add more paths across the circle, if desired.

PLAY THE GAME

1. Choose one person to be the fox and assign the others to be geese.

2. Players may only move along the paths.

3. The fox chases the geese along the paths.

4. If the fox catches a goose, that person also becomes a fox.

5. Keep playing until everyone becomes a fox.

KEEP IT WILD

Fox and Geese is a game that originated during Colonial times. It's a type of tag game that is played by making tracks to create paths in snow. Try fox walking as slowly and silently as you can. How close can you get to a squirrel or bird?

 EXTENDING THE EXPERIENCE

Want to see more animal tracks? Make a hidden feeding station on the ground. Fill a shallow tray with birdseed, nuts, and berries.

ICE

NATURE PLAY EXPERIENCE

Take a walk through the winter landscape. What do you notice? Are trees glistening with ice? Is there frost on the leaves and on fern fronds? Do you see animal tracks in frozen ground or on snow? Are icicles beginning to form? Imagine you are in a sparkling, magical land!

MAKE IT WILD: SPARKLING ICE VILLAGE

Gather some natural objects to use to create your own sparkling ice village.

MATERIALS

〉 Various recycled containers
〉 Water
〉 Natural objects (berries, nuts, seeds, pine needles, leaves, plants)
〉 Food coloring or liquid watercolors
〉 Paintbrushes
〉 Salt shakers

PROCESS

1. Freeze water and natural objects in various molds and recycled containers. This can be done in your freezer if space allows, or overnight outdoors if the temperature is below freezing.

2. Invite friends to an icy playdate. Ask them to bring their own special ice blocks. This is especially fun to do in snow—don't forget a thermos of hot cocoa!

3. At the playdate, work together outdoors to build a village with the ice blocks.

4. Splash colors onto the ice with paintbrushes dipped into food coloring or watercolors.

5. Experiment with salt by sprinkling it onto the ice. What do you notice as you build with the ice? Is the salt useful in any way?

6. Warm up with some cocoa.

KEEP IT WILD

Any water can freeze into ice if the temperature is 32°F (0°C) or below, from small, shallow puddles to ponds and lakes. Observe ice on a winter walk. Where do you notice the most ice? Least? Don't walk on ice that is fewer than 4 inches (10 cm) thick—ask an adult about walking or skating on ice before you try it.

 EXTENDING THE EXPERIENCE

Try freezing natural objects such as berries, seeds, and leaves in small food molds or muffin tins filled with water to create winter suncatchers. Before freezing, add a vine clipping, ribbon, or piece of twine so you will be able to hang your suncatchers outside.

FORAGING

NATURE PLAY EXPERIENCE

As winter winds down and the days become warmer, tree sap begins to flow. Many types of trees can be tapped because they produce sap that contains enough sugar to be made into syrup. The best time to collect the sap is when the days become warmer (above 32°F [0°C]) but the nights are still cold (dipping below freezing temperatures). This repeated freezing and thawing builds pressure in the tree so when the tree is tapped, the sap flows out. Ideal trees to tap include sugar maple, red maple, silver maple, Norway maple, sycamore, and black walnut.

If you have access to maple, sycamore, or walnut trees, you can tap them and make your own syrup! You can even use a combination of sap from various trees to make your own unique flavor. Here is what you will need for tapping: a drill, $7/16$-inch (11 mm) drill bit, spile (tap with spout), metal bucket with lid, and hook for hanging.

Note: Follow a local maple sugaring forum to find the best times for tapping trees.

MAKE IT WILD: MAPLE SYRUP

It takes a lot of tree sap to make syrup—40 gallons (150 L) in fact, just to make 1 gallon (4 L) of syrup! After tapping the trees and harvesting the sap, try your hand at making your own syrup.

MATERIALS

> **10 gallons (38 L) sap**
> **Strainer**
> **Stainless-steel cooking pots/pans**
> **Fire pit with a cooking setup or propane stove**
> **Skimmer**
> **Syrup thermometer**

PROCESS

1. Pour the sap through a strainer into the cooking pot.

2. Outdoors, boil the pot over fire or on propane stove until the sap begins to thicken and becomes a light amber color, skimming foam every 30 minutes or so.

3. Pour the sap into smaller pot and finish it over the stove indoors, boiling until the sap becomes syrup (between 215°F and 219°F [102°C to 104°C]).

4. Pour the syrup into a glass jar or bottle.

5. Store the syrup in the refrigerator.

Note: The sap can be divided into more than one cooking pot to reduce the boiling time. Ten gallons (38 L) divided into thirds will take about 3½ hours.

KEEP IT WILD

Trees should be at least 18 inches (45 cm) in diameter for one tap. Trees up to 24 inches (60 cm) can hold two taps. Remember to ask permission to tap trees that are not your own.

EXTENDING THE EXPERIENCE

Make fluffy buttermilk or banana pancakes to eat with your tasty syrup!

SHELTER

NATURE PLAY EXPERIENCE

Just as people seek solace from the cold, other animals seek cozy places to stay warm and dry. Not all animals migrate to a warmer place or hibernate to rest in winter. Some animals are dormant during cold snaps but awaken on mild winter days to forage before returning to slumber again. Survey the surroundings during a winter hike. If you were a mouse, where would you go to find shelter?

MAKE IT WILD: BRUSH PILE

This quick shelter will give small animals shelter from the cold.

MATERIALS

> Fallen branches
> Leaves and dried grasses

PROCESS

1. Gather branches that have freshly fallen from trees.

2. Make a pile of branches by loosely stacking them.

3. Add leaves and dried grasses to the pile.

KEEP IT WILD

Hang a bird feeder close to the brush pile—little creatures will use the shelter as they go back and forth to feed.

EXTENDING THE EXPERIENCE

Make a milk carton feeder for your feathered friends! Cut panels out of all four sides of a clean half-gallon (1.9 L) milk carton, leaving a 2- to 3-inch (5 to 8 cm)-deep bowl at the bottom for birdseed. You can lightly sand and paint the carton with acrylic paints if you'd like. Cut small slits on opposite sides of the feeder, then poke a stick through to make a perch. Fill with seed and watch for birds to visit.

4

SEASONAL NATURE PLAY:
SPRING

After a long winter, spring may seem slow to arrive. But with more sunlight and warming soil, plants sprout and animals awaken from their slumber. A show of color, scent, and song fills the air. For many, spring is a hopeful time, a promise of warmer days kept in earnest after a cold winter. We sense spring's energy in the fresh colors that burst forth on bird feathers, tree buds, and colorful blooms. Spring is a time to plant seeds, smell the flowers, watch for the return of migrating animals, and observe new life that surrounds us.

SPRING RETURNS

by Monica Wiedel-Lubinski

Warm earth warms up little seeds
That have waited through the cold.
Tiny sprouts unfurl their leaves with
Winter secrets to be told.
Buds cupped tightly, ready now,
As petals stretch for sun.
Fragrant blossoms on the bough
Tell winged friends the time has come.
Sweet flowers whisper it is spring,
To every leaf and paw and wing.
Frogs and birds begin to sing,
Spring breathes life back into being.

CHANGING SKY

NATURE PLAY EXPERIENCE

Go outside on a windy day to investigate which way the wind blows. Begin by closing your eyes. Feel the wind on your skin and notice how it blows your hair. Which direction does it seem to be blowing from? Open your eyes and look around. Is the wind blowing objects nearby? Is the wind moving through grasses or rustling the leaves?

Note: Wind is the movement of air created by pressure in the atmosphere, which is caused by uneven heating of the Earth's surface (such as when warm and cool air collide).

MAKE IT WILD: RECYCLED PAPER KITE

Ride the wind with a homemade kite!

MATERIALS

> 2 thin, sturdy sticks with outer bark peeled off (one stick should be slightly longer than the other)
> Pocket knife
> Twine
> Recycled newspaper or gift tissue paper in a large sheet
> Ribbon

PROCESS

1. Form a T with the two sticks to make a frame.
2. Notch the longer stick about a quarter of the way down where the crossbar (shorter stick) will attach.

3. Tie the sticks in place with twine and finish with a double knot.

4. Lay the frame onto your paper; trace and cut out the sail.

5. Use twine to tie the paper sail to the frame on all four corners of the frame.

6. Tie a smaller secondary piece of twine onto each side of the crossbar, leaving enough slack to attach the longer kite string (see picture).

7. Tie the end of the kite string onto the lower portion of the longer main part of the frame. Then lift up the secondary piece of twine and tie the kite string to the center of the secondary piece of twine. The result will be a kind of twine pyramid that will help you guide your kite when flying (see picture).

8. Attach a ribbon for a tail to help balance the weight of the kite.

9. Head out on a windy day and see how it flies!

KEEP IT WILD

Many animals are on the wing in spring. Use your Natural Events Calendar (see page 131) to note when you spot the first migrating birds and butterflies in your region.

 ## EXTENDING THE EXPERIENCE

A wind sock or even a ribbon on the breeze can point you in the right direction if you'd like to know which way the wind blows. Use a pocket compass or phone app to determine the direction of the wind.

SPROUTS AND BLOSSOMS

NATURE PLAY EXPERIENCE

Take a closer look at the tips of branches on nearby trees and shrubs. What do you notice? Are fat buds about to burst open? Are tiny, sun-catching leaves catching your eye in shades of bright yellow-green? Explore the forest to find sprouts and fresh, young blossoms. What scents are present? What colors are popping? Bring along your nature journal to record the bloom times of plants you discover or to make sketches of interesting plants you find.

MAKE IT WILD: PLANTING SEEDS

You can grow plants in eggshells and transplant them into your garden. It's up to you what to grow! Fruits, vegetables, herbs, and wildflowers are all great choices.

MATERIALS

- Cardboard egg carton with the top removed and stacked underneath
- 12 eggshells (shells should be intact enough to put soil inside)
- Potting soil
- Compost (optional)
- Seeds
- Dish towel
- Water

Note: If you don't have eggshells, you can put soil directly into the egg carton. When you're ready to transplant seedlings, just cut each section of the carton and plant it directly into soil.

PROCESS

1. Place eggshells in each section of the egg carton.

2. Fill each eggshell with potting soil; amend the soil to enrich with compost, if you have it.

3. Sow seeds in the eggshells and gently cover with soil as indicated on the seed package.

4. Find a sunny windowsill for your egg carton.

5. Fold a dish towel and place it on the windowsill, then place the egg carton planter on top.

6. Lightly water the seeds. Let the soil dry completely between each watering to prevent too much moisture.

7. Watch seeds sprout and grow! Use the Seedling Growth Chart found in chapter 7 (page 139) if you'd like to track growth.

Note: Seeds need different amounts of light, soil, and nutrients depending on the plant. Many seeds also need a cold spell to "harden" before sprouting, which simulates what happens in winter. Read about the conditions your seeds need before you plant them.

KEEP IT WILD

Flowering plants like garlic mustard (*Alliaria petiolata*) and dandelions (*Taraxacum officinale*) are prolific and easy to find in spring. The young leaves of either plant are also tasty in spring salads.

EXTENDING THE EXPERIENCE

Gather and plant a range of tree seeds to see which ones will grow. Acorns, maple seeds, beechnuts, walnuts, and even pinecones can sprout and eventually become trees.

RAIN

NATURE PLAY EXPERIENCE

Spring is a wonderful time to feel the rain. Whether it is a gentle passing shower or steady rainfall, you are sure to be energized by this sensory experience! Gear up and explore the glistening landscape. Touch wet leaves and grass. Search for dry patches protected by foliage. If you were a bird or bee, where might you hide? Can you spy worms that have emerged from the saturated soil? Follow the watery paths of intermittent streams made by the rain. Where does the water go? Which direction does it flow?

MAKE IT WILD: MUD PIES

Like to get messy? Then try your hand at making mud pies!

MATERIALS

> Pail, beach bucket, or clean recycled containers
> Shovel, spoon, or stick for digging
> Flat cooking sheet, muffin tin, or pie pan (optional)

PROCESS

1. Find a muddy patch of ground where you have permission to dig.
2. Scoop and dig mud to your delight.
3. Fill the pail with mud and rain. Mix in any other natural objects you'd like for your "pie."

4. Roll and pat mud into mud pies or other muddy treats.

5. "Bake" and serve mud pies!

KEEP IT WILD

The water cycle is fascinating. Select a puddle and observe it over several days as the water evaporates in dry conditions. Where does the water go?

 ## EXTENDING THE EXPERIENCE

Make a mud pie café! All you need is a muddy place to dig and some repurposed kitchen items such as bowls and spoons. If you have stumps, logs, or crates, you can build tables for making and serving creations from your muddy menu.

MUSHROOMS AND MOSS

NATURE PLAY EXPERIENCE

Take a nature walk or visit a natural area where you are likely to find fungi. As you explore, look around the base of trees, on fallen logs, and in moist soil for these interesting organisms. What do you wonder about fungi and moss you find? (Although moss and fungi can be found any time of year, spring usually yields the perfect growing conditions.)

While playing among the mushrooms, mind your step so as not to harm them. You may even find a fairy ring! What do you notice about the habitat where fungi and moss are found? The feel of moss is soft, velvety, and wonderful. Gently explore moss with your fingers and toes. How do you think nearby animals might rely on mushrooms, lichens, or moss? What animal clues can you find nearby?

MAKE IT WILD: MUSHROOM AND MOSS PRINTING WITH NATURAL PAINT

After a woodland wander to locate mushrooms and moss, you can collect some for printmaking. Delicately harvest only a few bits of moss and/or fungi that are pleasing to you. Make your own paint and then have fun creating your nature prints!

MATERIALS

> 1 cup (150 g) flour

> 1 cup (150 g) salt

> 1 cup (250 ml) warm water

> Food coloring or liquid watercolors

> Harvested moss, mushrooms, lichen

> Thick paper (such as watercolor paper or card stock)

PROCESS

1. Make the paint by mixing flour, salt, and water until smooth. Add more water as needed to achieve a smooth, paint-like consistency. Mix in a few drops of color. Now your paint is ready.

2. Gently dip mushrooms or moss into your paint and press them onto paper like a stamp. Try the mushrooms gill-side down, or if it is small enough, dip the entire mushroom. Have fun experimenting!

3. Try making various colors of paint, matching them to your fungi and moss. You can store extra paint in the refrigerator for up to 1 week. When you're finished, return the natural materials back to the earth outside.

KEEP IT WILD

Many mushrooms are not good for humans to eat and some are even poisonous. On the other hand, most fungi provide an important food source for animals. To protect fungi and moss, only collect a few samples where they are plentiful. To protect yourself, do not eat anything that you cannot identify with certainty!

 ## EXTENDING THE EXPERIENCE

Consider using leaves, acorn caps, evergreen needles, tree bark, or other fallen nature treasures to make your nature prints. As a process-based art experience, emphasis should be on experimentation with the paint and textures of the materials, not on creating a perfect final product.

WATERWAYS

NATURE PLAY EXPERIENCE

Visit a pond or stream to discover what lives there. Where is the water moving fast or barely at all? Are any creatures visible at first glance? Gently turn over a rock to see if anything clings to the underside or swims away. Are there jelly-like eggs on the water? Do you hear frogs splashing to safety in the leaves at the bottom of the pond? Notice the diversity of life found in this aquatic habitat. What plants are unique to the water's edge? How do they differ from other plants on higher ground?

MAKE IT WILD: WALNUT BOATS

This engineering challenge is harder than you think! Experiment with the weight of items used to make your boat (mud, leaf, and twig), then float your boat in a nearby stream or pond.

MATERIALS

> Walnuts
> Nutcracker
> Lump of mud, clay, or play dough
> Leaf
> Twig

PROCESS

1. Crack the walnuts and remove the nut inside. Use hollow half of each walnut to make a boat.

2. Roll mud or clay into a ball and press inside each walnut half.

3. Tear a small hole at top and bottom of a leaf, then insert a twig through the leaf to make a sail.

4. Place the twig with its leaf sail upright in the mud inside the boat.

5. See how far you can float your boat!

KEEP IT WILD

Whether you explore on land or in the water, make sure you only leave footprints behind.

EXTENDING THE EXPERIENCE

There are several aquatic species like dolphins, eels, sharks, and salmon that return to the same waterways each year to mate and feed (another form of migration). Plan a special canoe trip or stream search at a local nature center to learn more about the amazing aquatic native animals near you.

CALLS AND SONGS

NATURE PLAY EXPERIENCE

Find a favorite outdoor setting to sit and listen to the sounds of spring. Edge habitats (where brushy areas meet open fields or forests) are good places to start because they provide food and shelter for birds. Sit as still as you can and listen closely for a few moments. What sounds do you hear? How do the sounds change the longer you quietly sit? Could any of these sounds be harsh warning calls? Do you hear whistles, trills, or flute-like songs as animals call for mates? Try mimicking the calls and songs!

MAKE IT WILD: SOUND SHAKERS

This game will help hone your listening skills which is not only fun, but also useful as you learn to identify birds by sound.

MATERIALS

> **3 toilet paper tubes, cut in half to make 6 shakers**
> **Repurposed gift tissue paper**
> **Scissors**
> **12 rubber bands**
> **Assorted objects such as pebbles, seeds, and bottle caps**

PROCESS

1. Cut the tissue paper into 3-by-3-inch (8 by 8 cm) squares. You'll need twelve.

2. Place a tissue paper square onto one end of all six paper tubes and secure with a rubber band. Repeat for all six tubes.

3. Fill one tube with a few pebbles. Cover the open end with another paper square and securely wrap with a rubber band. Test how it sounds. Repeat with a second tube so that both shakers sound alike.

4. Repeat with remaining tubes until you have three pairs of shakers, each with matching sounds.

Note: You can double up the tissue paper to be sure that the objects don't rip the paper when you shake them.

PLAY THE GAME

Arrange the shakers randomly. The first player chooses a shaker, listens, and then selects another shaker. If the second shaker isn't a match, both shakers are returned to their original position. The next player chooses a shaker, listens, and tries to make a match. When one player makes a match, it's the next player's turn. Continue until all of the matches have been discovered. You can make the game more challenging by adding more sounds. This is a wonderful parallel to the way many animals rely on sound to find their mates.

KEEP IT WILD

Share your love of birds with others! Invite elders in your family, neighborhood, or local retirement community to watch and listen to the birds with you.

 # EXTENDING THE EXPERIENCE

As birdwatching interest grows, try to identify animals you hear by sound as well as by sight. You can learn identifying features of birds and frogs by using a field guide.

FORAGING

NATURE PLAY EXPERIENCE

At long last, plants unfurl tender buds and reveal lovely petals and fresh new leaves. Given the bounty of spring plants as producers of food, hungry consumers (animals that are omnivores, herbivores, and carnivores) take advantage of delicious new food sources. Hunting goes hand in hand with foraging as animals seek nourishment after a lean winter, dormancy, or migration. Animals are also looking to feed their young, so although spring is a time of plentiful food, foraging animals must remain on high alert. There are others ready to spring into action.

Frolic and play outdoors as you explore spring growth. What clues indicate that animals are awake and feeding on tasty flowers and leaves? Is there evidence of insects such as ants nibbling at flower buds? Do you notice flies, beetles, or bees visiting nearby flowers? Are there signs that rabbits or deer have foraged in your yard or park?

MAKE IT WILD: VIOLET JAM

Some flowers are beautiful to look at and to eat!
Make this delicious spring jam from foraged violets.

MATERIALS

⟩ 2–3 cups (680–1020 grams) violets

⟩ 2 ½ cups (570 ml) water

⟩ Colander

⟩ Cheesecloth or paper towel

⟩ 1 lemon

⟩ 4 (4-ounce [120 ml]) canning jars

⟩ 1 (1.75-ounce [50 g]) standard package Sure-Jell
fruit pectin

⟩ 3 cups (600 g) sugar, more or less to taste
(you can use as little as 2 cups [400 g] or as
much as 4 cups [800 g])

PROCESS

1. Go on a wander to gather violets where they are plentiful. (You can pick whole blossoms, but you won't need the stems.)

2. Place the violet flowers in a large, heat-safe mixing bowl. Rinse them and set aside.

3. Bring 2½ cups (570 ml) of water to a boil (a tea kettle is ideal).

4. Pour the boiling water over the violets.

5. Let the violets steep in the water until the color turns blue-violet. You can use the mixture as soon as the water is cool, or you can let it sit covered for up to 24 hours.

6. Strain the liquid through a colander lined with cheesecloth or paper towel, or strain through a mesh sieve to remove the flowers.

7. Squeeze the lemon. You should have about ¼ cup (60 ml) of juice. Add the juice to the strained liquid. (*Note: The color of the mixture has an instant reaction with the acid of the lemon juice when you pour it in—it's fun to see!*)

8. Sterilize the canning jars if you are processing for canning. Set them aside.

9. Follow the directions on the Sure-Jell package to make the jelly.

10. Whisk the pectin jam with the violet tea/lemon liquid. Stir over medium heat until it reaches a rolling boil.

11. Add the sugar while stirring constantly. Return to a boil and boil for 1 to 2 minutes to ensure ingredients are fully mixed.

12. Remove the jelly from the heat, skim off the foam, and ladle or pour into jars. If canning, place in a boiling water bath for 10 minutes. Let the jelly sit for 24 hours to ensure it is set and the flavor is infused throughout before serving.

KEEP IT WILD

People aren't the only ones excited about delicious food sprouting up! When you forage, take only what you need and use everything you take. Never forage where herbicides or pesticides are applied.

EXTENDING THE EXPERIENCE

Discover spring wild edibles in your region with an experienced naturalist or botanist. Your local nature center or botanical garden may offer free walks for families. Try foraging a green salad full of dandelion leaves, chickweed, violets, wood sorrel, blueberries, and spruce bud tips—whatever is plentiful near you.

NESTS

NATURE PLAY EXPERIENCE

Many animals are masterful engineers, not least of all birds! Take a spring walk to observe birds making nests. See if you can spy any of these scenarios:

- a bird carrying grass
- a bird carrying sticks or twigs
- a bird carrying mud
- a bird carrying a feather
- a bird pair working on a nest
- a bird flying in and out of a tree cavity
- a bird pair feeding babies in a nest

What else are the birds doing? Did this give you any clues about the birds that live here?

MAKE IT WILD: NEST HELPERS

We can help birds prepare for their young by offering a small supply of nesting materials.

MATERIALS

> Repurposed mesh produce bag
> Assortment of nesting materials such as wool, dried grass clippings, dried bark, pine needles, fluffy plant down, moss, animal fur, yarn scraps
> Twine

PROCESS

1. Fill your mesh produce bag with assorted natural materials.

2. Pull a few of the materials through the mesh to make it easier for birds to quickly grab them

3. Hang the nest helper with twine where you can observe birds at work!

KEEP IT WILD

Only offer natural fiber nesting materials. Don't offer dryer lint, plastics, or aluminum foil.

EXTENDING THE EXPERIENCE

Many birds will use birdhouses or hollow gourds to make their nests. Hang birdhouses to welcome them to your yard! Learn more about bird conservation efforts and volunteer to help with bird banding or citizen science projects that monitor local bird populations.

5

YEAR-ROUND
NATURE PLAY

Nature play can happen in every season. With ample time outside, children become attuned to subtle changes that occur throughout the year. For most people, dramatic natural events like a thunderstorm or an influx of cicadas calling is impossible to miss. But a more nuanced understanding of nature's inner workings happens in many small moments of wonder. The greater the frequency of outdoor play—in all seasons—the more likely children are to develop a deeper nature connection.

THE SUN COMES UP

inspired by Elizabeth Mitchell's "Sunny Day," adapted by Karen Madigan and Monica Wiedel-Lubinski

The sun comes up *(the sun comes up)*

The rain comes down *(the rain comes down)*

The flowers bloom *(the flowers bloom)*

All around *(all around)*

The animals eat *(the animals eat)*

The children play *(the children play)*

The sun comes up *(the sun comes up)*

Another day.

COLLECTING NATURAL TREASURES

NATURE PLAY EXPERIENCE

Go on an outdoor walk. Observe the natural setting with a wide view, taking in the larger landscape. Notice features farthest away from you such as clouds, mountain tops, rock formations, trees, or cityscapes along the horizon. Gradually zoom in on smaller objects closer in your view. Freely explore and play in this habitat. If there are plentiful natural objects, use a small pail or egg carton to gather some of the treasures that have fallen to the ground. Do these objects make a sound? Or have a scent? Are the objects heavy or light in your hand?

Thoughtfully collect bits of natural materials that speak to you. These special collections can help you learn about the plants, animals, land, and seasons as they change.

MAKE IT WILD: TREASURE VINE

Gathered treasures can become records of time spent in nature. Whether it be a wilted flower, blade of dried grass, or delicate twig, follow your instincts about what to place in a keepsake treasure vine.

MATERIALS

> 2–3 feet (60–90 cm) harvested wisteria vine or other type of vine such as bittersweet, honeysuckle, or grapevine (you can use a Y-shaped branch in place of a vine if needed)
> Twine or other natural cordage
> Natural objects

PROCESS

1. Peel the outer layer of bark off the wisteria vine. It will come off in long strips that can also be used for cordage. Set aside the outer bark to work with the smooth vine.

2. Once peeled, bring the ends of the vine together to overlap and form a raindrop shape with the vine.

3. Use twine or cordage to securely tie the ends in place.

4. Tie off another length of twine at the top and begin wrapping it back and forth across the raindrop shape to create a freeform weave.

5. Gently tuck your objects into the weave.

6. Display and add to the treasure vine as often as you like!

KEEP IT WILD

Collecting feathers without a permit is prohibited by the US Migratory Bird Treaty Act. This law protects birds and prevents commercial trade in feathers, regardless of how they were obtained. Federally recognized Native American tribes have special permission to gather plants for traditional purposes. You can gather feathers for study but return them to nature when you are finished.

 ## EXTENDING THE EXPERIENCE

When looking back at the found treasures, jot down where you found each item in your nature journal. You could snap a picture to glue in or draw the items while reminiscing about your day.

LOOSE-PARTS AND SMALL-WORLDS PLAY

NATURE PLAY EXPERIENCE

Loose-parts play has been a star in the spotlight of early childhood education in recent years. However, the idea that children are actually learning by playing with random items goes back to the early 1970s, when an architect named Simon Nicholson wrote the article "How NOT to Cheat Children: The Theory of Loose Parts" and opened the minds of educators all over the world. We owe him a great deal of thanks for placing value on allowing children to investigate, explore, and experiment in any environment. Loose parts play offers endless possibilities for creativity, imagination, and invention.

Put on your collecting hat, grab a basket or bag, and head out in search of natural loose parts! Create a "loose-parts cache" outside where you can use these treasures.

MAKE IT WILD: FAIRY HOUSE

Using your natural loose parts, your child can create small worlds to use in imaginative play. Small-worlds play refers to the common practice of building miniature shelters or habitats. The small scale helps children playfully process much larger settings and ideas about the world. One type of small-worlds play is building a fairy house.

MATERIALS

> Sticks
> Mud
> Bark
> Stones
> Pinecones

> Acorn caps
> Moss
> Berries

PROCESS

1. Find a spot near the base of a tree, among ferns, or near other tall plants. Poke sticks into the ground to build the frame of your fairy house. Add mud and bark for siding, carpet it with moss, and use stones to make a walkway.

2. Embellish with pinecones, acorn caps, and more. Enjoy your fairy house with your favorite fairy dolls!

KEEP IT WILD

Fairies, also called faeries or fay, are magical creatures referenced in folklore all over the world. What special habitats or plants might fairies visit near you? Dream up and draw fairies in your nature journal or tell a story about a magical fairy adventure.

 ## EXTENDING THE EXPERIENCE

Abundant natural items are ideal for loose parts play, but just about anything can be used in building a collection of parts. Bottle caps, lids, corks, coffee cans, keys, and CDs are just some of the interesting things you can collect. Visit your local hardware store for items such as carpet and tile samples or paint swatches, which are usually free.

ROCKS

NATURE PLAY EXPERIENCE

Rocks seem to invite little hands to touch and play with them. Nature play with rocks can enhance physical development as children pick up tiny stones with fingers or carry around and pile up larger rocks. The colors, sizes, and textures of individual rocks are intriguing. Careful study of rocks can reveal what minerals or crystals are present, or if you have come upon a fossil. Perhaps you have a future geologist in your midst!

Visit a stream, beach, or other waterway where rocks and stones are plentiful and you can freely explore. Look under the rocks for insect larvae, snails, and other aquatic critters. You might even see salamanders or crayfish.

Note: The best rock hounds examine their finds in person with other experts. Visit your local natural science museum, gem and mineral club, or university geology department for help identifying your rocks.

MAKE IT WILD: WOOL FELTED ROCKS

Are there any rocks that look like they are wearing moss sweaters? Did you know you can make a sweater for a rock?

MATERIALS

- Wool roving
- River rocks or other smooth stones (such as from your local garden center)
- 2 large bowls or tubs
- Dish soap
- Warm water
- Cold water

PROCESS

1. Choose the perfect rock (it should feel good in your hand).
2. Wrap the rock thoroughly with wool roving in two layers (as shown). Do not leave any rock showing.

3. Fill a bowl or tub with warm water, add several drops of soap, and stir. Fill a separate bowl with cold water.

4. Gently cup the rock in both hands and dip it in the warm, soapy water.

5. Squeeze and pat the rock *very* lightly for several minutes until the wool begins to cling to the rock, dipping it back into the warm water occasionally.

6. Once the wool begins to cling and shrink around the rock, start to rub it between your hands, gently at first and becoming more vigorous as the wool tightens around the rock.

7. Continue to dip the rock in the warm water, then in cold water. Repeat dipping in both warm and cold water for several minutes while continuing to rub the wool between your hands.

8. When the wool has fully shrunken around the rock, rinse in cold water until the water runs clear.

9. Let the rock dry in the sun.

10. Enjoy your cozy sweater-wearing rock!

KEEP IT WILD

Be mindful of creatures that make their homes under stones in streams. If you lift a rock to look underneath, carefully place it back where you found it.

 EXTENDING THE EXPERIENCE

Use your felted rocks to build a totem or cairn. Turn it into a family game by taking turns stacking one rock at a time until the stack tumbles down. How many rocks were you able to stack?

STICKS

NATURE PLAY EXPERIENCE

Trees naturally lose limbs because of wind, insects, or disease. They replenish nutrients in the soil as they fall and decompose. They're also a reliable source of food and shelter for animals. When you take a walk, compare the sizes of branches on the ground. Notice the array of colors the bark can be. Challenge yourself to find ten different sticks of various sizes and colors. When you slow down to look closely, you may be surprised by the variety of sticks around you!

MAKE IT WILD: WHITTLED WOOD SCRIBE

Because sticks are plentiful, you might try your hand at whittling a scribe to use in your nature journal.

Note: An adult should closely supervise the use of sharp tools.

MATERIALS

> Sharp knife

> Sharpening stone

> Branch of soft wood such as pine, cedar, basswood, or spruce

> Scrap board or thick leather mat to protect your lap

> Gloves or a thumb guard

PROCESS

1. Select a suitable branch made of soft wood.

2. Establish a safe space (or "blood circle") that no one will enter while cutting.

3. Place a scrap board or mat on your lap. Wear gloves or a thumb guard.

4. Sharpen your knife on a sharpening stone (a dull knife is dangerous!).

5. Whittle one end of your branch until you create a pointed tip.

WHITTLING TIPS

〉 **Whittle along the grain of the wood.**

〉 **Stroke the knife blade away from your body with shallow, repetitive cuts.**

〉 **Remove the wood gradually, without making deep cuts.**

KEEP IT WILD

Save the wood shavings, as they are useful kindling for campfires.

 ## EXTENDING THE EXPERIENCE

Dip the scribe into homemade paint, mud, or ink and draw with it in your journal.

TREES

NATURE PLAY EXPERIENCE

Climbing a tree, like splashing in puddles and wishing on dandelion seeds, is a rite of passage. Climbing trees is risky play for sure, but with the freedom to try, and perhaps fail, and try again, we grow determined to navigate obstacles. Climbing trees builds perseverance and confidence as we rise to the challenge and succeed. It is exhilarating to perch in a tree!

Head to a park or nature center where there are trees ideal for climbing. You may want to start out by climbing on fallen logs first. Practice balancing and moving your body in different ways to scramble over logs. When you feel ready, select a tree to climb. You can do it! Trust your body and move slowly with each step. Don't ask a grown-up to put you up in a tree—it's important that you take time training your muscles for tree climbing on your own so that you'll be able to climb back down too.

What's it like up there? Can you see things you can't usually see from the ground? Is there anything in the tree, like a bird's nest, or even a bird?

Great Climbing Trees

⟩ Beech

⟩ Oak

⟩ Weeping willow

⟩ Mulberry

⟩ Fruit trees such as crabapple, apple, cherry, and pear

Safe Climbing Tips

⟩ Wear sturdy shoes with gripping soles and comfortable clothing.

⟩ Scope out the tree with an adult ahead of time to ensure it is safe for climbing.

⟩ Always have two hands on the tree and at least one foot.

⟩ Take your time.

⟩ Ask for help when you need it.

MAKE IT WILD: THROW A TREE PARTY!

Being among trees is a joyful and often magical experience. Trees give us such amazing gifts; why not celebrate these special living things? Invite your friends and family members to a tree party. After some fun tree climbing, make a leaf garland and decorate your favorite spot in the woods. Enjoy a picnic with snacks and tea, then dance around while singing to the treetops! Make notes about your day in your nature journal and remember to hug the trees!

MATERIALS

> Leaves
> Yarn or embroidery floss
> Embroidery needles
> Tablecloth or quilt
> Favorite snacks and tea
> Tea set

KEEP IT WILD

Scientists have been studying the phenomenon that trees can communicate with each other. They send underground signals through mycorrhizal networks. How cool!

EXTENDING THE EXPERIENCE

Invite friends and family to your tree party with handmade invitations. Perhaps you are inspired by the trees to make recycled paper (see paper-making instructions on page 113).

MUD

NATURE PLAY EXPERIENCE

What's more alluring than mud? It's wet, squishy, sloshy, and fun! Whether your child is a cautious observer or explores mud with his or her whole body, muddy nature play guarantees an adventure. Mud can be the medium for projects such as hand-rolled snakes or pinch pots. It can be the glue that binds projects engineered from natural materials like sticks and leaves. It can be painted to create thick, luscious works of art. Mud is also the magic ingredient in all sorts of "treats." Pies, muffins, cookies, and cakes are often baking in a mud-pie kitchen. Mud is a diverse art medium and is perfect for small-worlds play too.

Rainy-day walks mean splashing in puddles, playing in mud, and, if you're lucky, finding worms or other slimy creatures. Head out on a wet day outfitted with your rain gear in search of a muddy patch in the woods. Even without rain, mud is easy to make—you only need soil, water, and something to dig with.

MAKE IT WILD: NATURE FACES

Press mud onto tree bark, then sculpt a face with nearby natural materials. These nature faces can welcome forest visitors or be mysterious guardians in your neck of the woods.

MATERIALS

> Mud
> Trowel
> Small pails or containers
> Tree
> Various natural objects (acorns, seeds, berries, leaves, twigs)

PROCESS

1. Find a muddy spot where digging is allowed.
2. With trowel, collect some mud or soil in pails.
3. If necessary, mix in a little water to create a pliable consistency.
4. Use your hands to press mud onto a tree.
5. Form the mud into a rounded face shape.
6. Add natural items to make facial features.

KEEP IT WILD

Natural clays form along streambeds, riverbanks, and other sites where raw earth is exposed. With permission, you can gather clay for some sculpting fun. You can shape natural clay into functional or artistic creations, then let it bake in the sun or oven.

 ## EXTENDING THE EXPERIENCE

Why does mud dry out? Experiment with dried mud by soaking it in water. How long does it take for dry clumps of earth to return to soft, squishy mud? Experiment with different kinds of mud to see which dries out the quickest. You can also try painting with thin, watered-down mud. You'll be amazed at the range of colors mud paint can be. Add some natural dyes to expand your palette.

RECORDING NATURAL EVENTS

NATURE PLAY EXPERIENCE

The more you are outdoors, the more you will notice seasonal changes and interactions in the natural environment where you live. As a keen observer, recording these changes is a way to document what happens and compare your records from day to day, month to month, or even year to year. As you explore nature together, be on the lookout for these natural occurrences.

TEN NATURAL EVENTS TO LOOK FOR

> When do the frogs start to call in spring? Which ones?

> When does a particular bird species return from migration or begin to nest?

> What day does Jack Frost arrive?

> When does the first snowflake fall or a blizzard take place?

> When do you wear your mittens for the first time as the weather turns cold?

> Do salamanders or fish spawn at the same time and place predictably?

> When does a favorite wild berry ripen or wildflower bloom?

> When is the first barefoot warm day?

> Which butterfly is the first to emerge in spring?

> What surprising plant or animal did you discover on a given day?

MAKE IT WILD: NATURAL EVENTS CALENDAR

Use the template in chapter 7 to record your events. You can choose from either a monthly or yearly approach to your observations.

KEEP IT WILD

There are four astronomical seasons (summer, autumn, winter, and spring) that begin on a solstice or equinox. Consult the *Farmer's Almanac* to see how farmers rely on seasonal observations.

EXTENDING THE EXPERIENCE

The science of phenology is the study of cycles of plants and animals and the interconnected way that timing of these cycles relates to seasons and climate. Phenology is arguably the oldest branch of environmental science with records dating to 705 CE noting bloom times of cherry trees in Japan. Patterns of migration, spawning, bloom times, hibernation, rainfall, and more help us utilize natural resources (for example, farming and gardening) and better understand human impact on climate change. You can learn more about phenology through the writings of Aldo Leopold, Henry Thoreau, and Rachel Carson.

USING A NATURE JOURNAL

NATURE PLAY EXPERIENCE

Journaling is a personal way for people to express themselves. For some, journals are used to express thoughts and emotions by writing about a meaningful experience. Others jot down sentence fragments, capture fleeting ideas, or write poetry. Drawing, painting, and collage can also capture memories, especially of nature experiences.

For young children, the latter may be all they can do until they acquire the skills to write letters and words and begin to show interest in writing. Long before children are able to form letters or shapes, they can make marks. Mark making is an important part of children's motor development, eye-hand coordination, and spatial awareness.

Nature journaling is a creative way to encourage expression and reflection with or without the use of written words. Each nature experience is an opportunity to notice shapes, colors, patterns, textures, symmetry, and more! Below are some unique ways to use a nature journal:

> Trace or make rubbings of leaves, feathers, bark, and grasses.

> Glue dried leaves, seeds, moss, or flower petals inside.

> Press natural objects like flowers and leaves.

> Smoosh berries to find seeds or experiment with color.

> Paint with natural dyes and paintbrushes.

> Draw or paint with sticks or feathers dipped in mud, paint, or dye.

> Draw with charcoal from a cooled campfire or fireplace.

MAKE IT WILD: RECYCLED NATURE JOURNAL

There are some fantastic journals out there that can be purchased but making your own journal from recycled paper is easy and fun! It's also an opportunity to clue children in to where paper comes from and the importance of recycling. Not to mention this is a messy, sensory, and highly rewarding process! With just a few household items, you can make sheets of paper to bind together into a journal. Head outside with your materials and get busy.

MATERIALS

> **Paper scraps such as newspaper, construction paper, and tissue paper**
> **Large tub**
> **Water**
> **Manual handheld mixer**
> **Framed screen (or a piece of screen with edges covered by duct tape)**
> **Bath towels**
> **Piece of felt slightly smaller than screen**

PROCESS

1. Place the paper in the tub and tear it into small pieces.
2. Pour warm water over the paper until just covered.
3. Let it soak for several hours or overnight.
4. Have fun smooshing the paper with your hands and blending it with a hand-mixer to make a pulp. It should be a milkshake consistency.
5. Add enough warm water to allow the framed screen to be dipped into the tub.
6. Stir the pulp and water gently.
7. Dip the screen into tub and allow the pulp to settle on the screen.
8. Lift the screen out of tub and allow the water to drain.
9. Set the screen on a towel, place the felt on top of the pulp, and gently press to squeeze out water.
10. Flip the screen over and gently peel the paper off.
11. Place the paper on a dry towel and leave overnight.
12. Repeat for the number of pages you'd like in your journal.

When you have your sheets of paper, assemble them together into a book using a hole punch and twine, raffia, ribbon, or cordage. Decorate as desired!

Note: Dark-colored scraps will yield darker paper. The size of your screen will determine the size of the paper.

KEEP IT WILD

Paper is made from plant fibers, most often from softwood conifers including spruce, balsam fir, Eastern white pine, or hemlocks because they have long, strong fibers. Other plants like bamboo, hemp, eucalyptus, and cotton can also be used.

 ## EXTENDING THE EXPERIENCE

Jazz up your handmade paper by adding flower petals, small leaves, liquid watercolors, or tiny shape cutouts before lifting out the pulp. If you embed seeds into your paper, you can make notecards that can be planted.

6

VOICES FROM
THE FIELD

Seasoned nature-based educators share wisdom about more ways adults can explore nature with children. Many tips and ideas are offered here, often closely linked with a child's development, social interactions, and personal connections with nature. You'll receive guidance on the role of caring adults as children build confidence and hone the ability to assess risk during outdoor play. Some of these voices are educators as well as parents, which provides tempered insight about the dual role parents have as their child's first teacher. These activities and gentle suggestions come from professionals who specialize in facilitating outdoor learning with children. Read on for more fun ways to explore nature as a family!

Much more could be said on important topics such as equitable access to safe wild spaces, considerations for children with diverse needs and abilities, acknowledgment of indigenous cultures, and native ways of knowing the land. While we can't cover all of the topics and barriers that concern families in one book, the voices that follow have touched on a few of these topics with thoughtful insight to help frame parents' understanding. We encourage you to use the resources at the back of the book to learn more.

NEW TO OUTDOOR PLAY?

MORE IDEAS AND TIPS FOR PARENTS

SUSIE WIRTH, OUTREACH DIRECTOR (RETIRED)

Arbor Day Foundation and Dimensions Foundation

I'm often asked how families can bring more nature into their children's lives in their own backyards. My answer is, "Keep things simple." Nature play is not about knowing the name of every plant or animal but about having shared observations, discoveries, and fun. It *is* helpful to have a green space, no matter how small, with more diversity than just a lawn.

Here are a few inexpensive tips for families wanting to develop a nature-rich backyard space that is engaging for children:

- Create a cozy green nook where children can have imaginary play. Together you can build a sturdy teepee frame and plant vines (gourds or beans) around the perimeter, which soon will grow up over the frame. Or plant a small tree (such as a dwarf redbud) or a couple of adjacent shrubs to establish a shady, child-size space.
- Provide plenty of natural materials (age-appropriate-size shells, acorns, seedpods, stones, and so on) that children can use in creative ways.
- Devote a space to larger, natural materials where children use stump sections, logs, sturdy branches, or big tree cookies to build their own forts or castles. Make sure to have a soft layer of wood chips here.
- With your child, plant fragrant herbs and flowers that have diverse colors, sizes, and bloom times. If space allows, provide a small raised-bed garden where children can dig in the soil, planting and tending whatever flowers or vegetable appeals to them.

Most importantly, foster your child's sense of wonder and creativity. Ask open-ended questions. Invite them to tell you what they see, hear, smell, and feel. Encourage them to tell you what they like in the space. Follow their lead.

To get started, families can find free, easy-to-use, developmentally appropriate activities shown to engage families in exploring the natural world together at natureexplore.org/family-resources.

YASH BHAGWANJI, ASSOCIATE PROFESSOR OF EARLY CHILDHOOD EDUCATION

Florida Atlantic University, Boca Raton, Florida

Last spring, during an exploration of a nearby scrub habitat with my undergraduate students, we came upon a "fuzzy" looking creature on the trail. The students huddled around the creature and the conversation among the twelve or so students and myself went something like this:

Is it dead? Maybe it is playing dead. It's dead. Yes, it's dead. What is it? A squirrel? A mammal of some kind? Looks like a rat. Let's check the guidebook. Also check internet. It's an eastern mole. I wonder why it's dead. Could be the cold spell we had last night. There may be other eastern moles living here. Should we move it aside? Let's leave it there. It will decompose and turn to soil. Or something else might eat it.

As described above, adult caregivers such as parents, grandparents and kin, friends and neighbors, and teachers alike may all initiate journeys of empowering children and inspiring discovery of the caretaking process by first being in and learning about nature. The following habits or routines are recommended:

Being with Nature. Places of nature can be backyards, gardens, nearby ponds, wooded areas, parks, different types of habitats, nearby natural areas, and more. Nature is all around us—it is the fields, streams and rivers, clouds and sky, puddles after rain, groves of trees, shrubs and bushes, and bees and wasps buzzing around grasses and weeds—in fact, nature can be found anywhere where life finds an opportunity to grow. Being with nature also means an extensive amount of time is spent *in* and *together with* nature. A great way to *be* with nature is for caregivers and children to make frequent outings in nature a routine part of daily life.

Enjoyment in Being Part of Nature. This simply means children are provided with plenty of unstructured time and experiences *in* and *with* nature. Enjoyment occurs when children directly engage in all kinds of firsthand sensory experiences and discovery of the small and big ideas related to nature. And through easygoing conversations, caregivers should plan to support the development of children's kinship with nature too. The development of kinship with nature is specifically supported when caregivers emphasize or explain the value of nature in enabling cycles/processes of life and mutual benefits among many types of life forms.

PETER DARGATZ, KINDERGARTEN TEACHER

Woodside Elementary School, Sussex, Wisconsin

Let the child lead. While it is your duty to keep your child safe, it is not your duty to save them from risk. You might cringe a little the first time you see your child jump off a stump. Your heart might skip a beat the first time they pick up a stick. Your parental instincts might kick in and you will want to intervene or "teach" them about what to do. Bite your tongue. They can do much more than we give them credit for when out in nature. They are amazing risk assessors, creative thinkers, and problem solvers. But unless we let them hone their skills independently, they will never reach their fullest potential. Use a hands-off, eyes-on approach. Be present and positive and enjoy the things your child will teach you.

BETH SAVITZ, HEAD OF PARENT AND CHILD PROGRAMS

Irvine Nature Center, Owings Mills, Maryland

Connecting your toddler with nature can be very simple even if you don't live near a natural setting or have much money to spend:

- Make binoculars from cardboard tubes and head outdoors to watch birds.
- Create a simple bird feeder with a pinecone, nut butter, and birdseed. Hang it near your home to attract birds or even a hungry squirrel.
- Create a leaf rubbing by putting a leaf under a piece of paper and rubbing with the flat side of a crayon. Toddlers love to see the leaf magically appear!
- Make a nature scavenger hunt or find one online. Then head outdoors with an empty egg carton or other recycled container to collect your finds.
- Use the natural treasures that you find to create a feely box, nature journal, or collage.
- Search for signs of animals like tracks, scat, partially eaten nuts or leaves, feathers, fur, nests, holes in trees or the ground, bones, shells, or antlers.
- Collect and observe insects, amphibians, invertebrates, or aquatic life, then return the critters back where you found them.
- Take a night hike and listen to the sounds or gaze at the night sky.
- Visit the library to find books about aspects in nature that your or your child love. Then find a quiet outdoor space to read together.

NATURE PLAY AND CHILD DEVELOPMENT

PETER DARGATZ

Research is clear about the positive impacts experiences with nature play have on whole-child development. When it comes to socialization and the skills involved with relationship building, nature play is a wonderful equalizer.

A few years back, I was honored to have a student in my class who was on the autism spectrum. For much of the year, he struggled with peer relationships. In the traditional classroom, he often played alone, sometimes by his own choice but often because of failed social interactions with his peers. He struggled to read social cues and often put his own wants and desires ahead of those of his peers and our agreed-upon class expectations. While his demeanor was generally happy, it was evident that he thirsted for positive peer interactions.

He quenched this thirst in our outdoor classroom. When given the chance to be in child-led nature play, not only did he interact with his peers more frequently and more positively, others sought him out because of his creativity and leadership qualities. Even though I aim for my classroom to be inclusive and collaborative, he still saw it as "my classroom." He knew nature was for everyone, so there was no battle for control or any need to live up to anyone's expectations. He could simply be himself. He used his love for engineering to create construction scenarios with one of our space's fallen trees. Deeming himself the "foreman" of the forest, he worked well with his peers on different electrical, plumbing, and design projects, transforming the tree into a skyscraper. Slowly but surely, these transferred to the indoor classroom. Though he still struggled at times interpreting social cues, he became a more vocal part of our classroom discussions, initiated play independently, and accepted ideas and suggestions from others, even when he disagreed with them. In his mind, his skyscraper towered in the forest. In reality, his social skills were what grew to new and impressive heights.

BETH SAVITZ

The natural world provides limitless opportunities for toddlers to stretch their wings and learn to fly! Not only is nature's playground free, but it also offers a huge variety of spaces and structures for physical development and full-on fun.

Ways to Improve Gross Motor Skills

- Walk on a fallen log to practice balance.
- Lift or roll logs, rocks, and branches to build upper-body strength.
- Jump, climb, crawl on, or navigate around fallen logs to engage large muscle groups.
- Climb trees, hike, or run to build leg strength and locomotor coordination.
- Wade in shallow water to encourage balance on varied terrain.
- Shovel or rake dirt and sand, or using sweep nets to collect insects and engage arm muscles.
- Act out animal movements through pretend play to support whole-body motor skill development.

Ways to Improve Fine Motor Skills

- Use fingers to pick up natural items such as rocks, nuts, leaves, flowers, and feathers.
- Use hands to build a fairy house or create a nature mandala.
- Stack sticks or arrange them from smallest to largest.
- Cut grass or flowers with scissors.
- Squeeze, build, or paint with mud.
- Hold or touch worms, snails, salamanders, or toads.
- Use a magnifying lens or binoculars to observe natural elements.

MARISA SOBOLESKI, FOREST SCHOOL COORDINATOR
New Mexico School for the Deaf, Santa Fe and Albuquerque, New Mexico

Opportunities to play in nature offer plenty of benefits for all children, including stronger immune systems, increased attention, and memory. Within our general population, many marginalized groups gain from experiences in nature just as much as atypically developing children, perhaps more. What is considered supplementary for most is likely necessary for deaf children.

I am a deaf educator, a part-time homesteader, herbalist, forager, seed saver, and a mother of two children, one who is also deaf. I run a forest school program once a week and a school garden, bringing our deaf students outside on a regular basis. Our forest preschool program is the only currently running program for deaf children in the United States, and one of two known internationally. Many of our deaf students have additional challenges such as behavior and attention issues, as well as cognitive and physical disabilities. Offering accommodations such as pre- and post-teaching, visual/tactile aids, maximizing on teachable moments, and access to incidental learning all support deaf/hard of hearing children in experiencing the outdoors through nature play.

Approximately 5 percent of the world population is deaf or has other types of hearing loss, and deaf children make up a very small percentage of that. More than 90 percent of deaf children are born to hearing parents. This often means that acquiring a new language is a task that is new to many families with deaf children. Learning sign language is a fundamental human right for deaf children; this offers them a foundation that is easily accessible to them from an early age. Those who acquire sign language young frequently have better skills for maintaining attention, controlling impulses, and organization.

The prevalence of depression, anxiety, and other mental health needs are more pronounced in the deaf community. A study of 1,900 adults by deaf developmental psychology researcher Dr. Poorna Kushalnagar shows a strong and clear link between early life adverse communication experiences and adulthood chronic illnesses in the deaf community. Furthermore, it has been shown that deaf adults who lack early language skills have difficulties integrating interpersonal skills later in life. The possible causes for the chronic disorders are ongoing language deprivation issues, social isolation, adverse childhood experiences, and persistent communication barriers. This leads to increased stress, attention issues, and impulsive behavior.

On top of that, lack of freedom appears more pronounced with deaf and/or disabled children, which means their opportunities to experience nature and unstructured play is exponentially reduced as compared to their hearing peers. The children seem to be often "bubble wrapped." This happens because of communication barriers, especially if their parents do not sign or communicate with them clearly. For example, hearing adults may assume that a deaf child may not be attuned to possible risks found in nature. Many children live at residential deaf schools, and their opportunities to experience and learn from risk through unstructured nature play may be reduced and limited.

Nature play offers tools for developing resilience and grit, along with tools for problem solving. In the natural world, positive emotions and mindfulness can come instinctively. Being outdoors helps children unwind, slow down, observe more, and be in tune with their sense of wonder. Nature is a fantastic teacher that offers the opportunity to become curious and ask questions about Earth and the life that it supports. During our forest school sessions, the small creek and mud kitchen is a favorite element, especially in the high desert. One day, one of our students noticed that the creek dried up. She quickly signed to me, upset, that there was no more water. Other students ran to her and reassured her that it was temporarily "away." This led to conversations in sign language about where water came from, where we could find water, and how we could conserve and protect this finite resource. This supported the children in their inquiry, reflection, creative problem solving, and initiative, all in their natural language.

Deaf children as a linguistic and cultural minority often offer perspectives that are outside the box when it comes to social issues. Their unique views on social issues can offer creative solutions to many problems that affect our world. Parents can help nurture nature play by offering deaf children access to nature and sign language. Strong access to both helps them thrive and become essential members of our society.

Access to wild spaces is just as much as a human right as access to sign language for deaf children. Nature play offers them the opportunity to become curious, be creative, and connect with their parents/caregivers and peers.

PATRICIA LEON, PROGRAM DIRECTOR, PARENT AND CHILD INSTITUTE

Miami Nature Playschool, North Miami, Florida

One of the benefits of nature-based programs is the wide-open spaces they provide for play. When there is great physical distance between children, they verbalize their needs to different members of their peer group instead of relying on communication with a teacher or parent. Because of proximity, teachers may be more inclined to put words in the children's mouths in indoor settings. But by contrast, open outdoor spaces necessitate the use of language with others because the play can span widely across the landscape.

Nature-based programs have other surprising benefits for dual-language learners: open-ended outdoor play lends itself to hearing, mimicking, and naturally attaining words in other languages. Language starts exploding! Unhurried exploration and freedom to play at their own pace means children have plenty of time to hear and pick up new languages. Just as children may learn the call of a familiar bird or frog through repetition, they also learn the names of animals in more than one language. When children are exposed to a variety of languages in a natural, no-pressure environment, language acquisition blossoms. They discover there are many ways to ask for help and express ideas to communicate with others. Just as animals have many languages and modes of communication, so do people in the communities that we live in. Thanks to unstructured nature-based learning, children have opportunities to assimilate concepts born from social play, language-rich environments, and quality time spent in nature.

LAUREN BROWN, DIRECTOR
**Asheville Farmstead School,
Candler, North Carolina**

I witnessed a moment of play between two students in one of our outdoor spaces called Pine Play. These students helped the Farmstead in the orchard by planting apple, pear, persimmon, and mulberry trees. It became a regular weekly task to check on and care for our new trees. During their play, these two students moved logs around to create a growing space and dug holes to plant fruit and nut trees. They found sticks to represent trees, planted these sticks, and then remembered that they needed water too. Following the imaginary planting, the students took turns monitoring the growth of their "trees." This allowed the students to call on each other to help look for pests, bring more water for the plants, and eventually help with the harvest. They worked hard to care for these new trees they had planted and used their imagination to water, check for pests, and pretend to harvest. Socially they had to navigate one another's emotional responses, compromise, work together, and effectively communicate. They were also working on gross and fine motor skills, all while soaking in the vitamin D.

GOING OUT IN THE COLD

SHEILA WILLIAMS RIDGE, DIRECTOR
Shirley G. Moore Lab School, Institute of Child Development, University of Minnesota, Minneapolis, Minnesota

Engaging in cold-weather play can be exhilarating and provide opportunities for a huge variety of activities. For families, building quinzees or snow forts is a wonderful and easy project, and there are ways to incorporate art, dramatic play, and large motor activity for children and adults. It can also be fun to extend this play into building multiple forts and talking about neighborhoods and communities. There are quinzee-making directions available online. Be sure to build them safely, and do not allow children to crawl on top of them when someone is inside.

Another fun cold-weather activity that I personally enjoy is sledding. For young children, you don't have to venture far or go to a designated sledding hill, just a small hill built out of what you shoveled from your driveway provides more than enough slope to make it fun.

The last cold-weather activity that I will share here is freezing colorful pieces of ice and using them to build outside on a small table. They work like ordinary blocks and can be used with snow or on their own. Just fill a variety of ice molds, add a few drops of food coloring or watercolor, and leave out overnight.

For any cold-weather play, the keys to enjoyment are engagement and comfort. Whether children are doing an activity at a table or building a large structure like a quinzee, they may experience different levels of warmth and comfort. Helping children understand their bodies and how to care for them is an important skill, and by listening to their concerns about heat or cold during outdoor play, we can help them learn to listen to what their bodies need. Often when I am building a snow fort with children, they get overheated and need to remove a layer or at least open a jacket. While doing a stationary project when it's cold, they may get cold feet or hands, so we can take a break and move around, or add some wool socks or warmer mittens.

Cold weather also allows children to think more broadly about their place and the world around them. They often ask questions like "Where are the birds when it's cold?" or "Is it spring yet?" when they see small plants starting to emerge. These experiences are key in developing a sense of place and understanding seasons and weather, and later they will be helpful for children to understand more complex issues like climate change.

Snow provokes responses that reach right back into childhood.
—Andy Goldsworthy

PAIGE VONDER HAAR, DIRECTOR
Bunnell House Early Childhood Lab School, Fairbanks, Alaska

Nature play helps form a child's sense of place, bonds them to the unique area where they reside, and provides time to develop appreciation for the natural world in all its transformations.

The intimate connection to place formed in childhood endures throughout life, often expressed in fond and emotive recollection. The children's book *Roxaboxen* by Alice McLerran represents this experience beautifully. Recall your own childhood and your nature memories specific to where you grew up. Did you wade in bubbling creeks and catch crayfish in your hands? Did you build forts from tumbleweeds? Your particular location afforded you the outdoor experiences of your childhood.

Winter is probably the most underappreciated season for outdoor play, but winter has its own unique richness, beauty, and learning opportunities. In winter, the environment is made over by crunchy leaves, frost, ice, and snow. Children view the outdoors through a new lens as they explore and imagine in a transformed world.

Whether children live near beaches, forests, rivers, ponds, fields, trails, deserts, or mountains will have an impact on their individual nature experiences. Children encouraged to venture outdoors in winter will be rewarded with the magical memories only winter can offer as they negotiate icy paths and snow-covered spaces; observe changes to the earth, water, and air; and discover the twinkling beauty of frost and the slushy cold of a winter puddle.

Exposure to and participation in traditional outdoor winter activities bond children to the culture around them and enhance children's development of a sense of place. For example, cross-country skiing, ice fishing, aurora borealis viewing, and dog mushing are prevalent winter activities in northern Alaska communities. Many children there both observe and participate in them. Activities unique to place—structured and unstructured—are valuable in helping form a child's understanding of the culture in which they live.

Nature play in winter is an essential experience for the well-rounded development of a child's sense of place. While it may take a little preparation, young children genuinely enjoy cold-weather play when they are dressed to be snug and dry yet are still able to move and navigate the winter environment. Winter is an amazing season. Dress children warmly and take them outdoors to explore and discover what winter uniquely offers!

NATURE PLAY IN URBAN SETTINGS

MONICA FRENCH, COFOUNDER AND DIRECTOR

Wild Haven Forest Preschool and Childcare, Baltimore, Maryland

Often when people think about connecting to nature, they picture themselves in wild, faraway places like forests, mountains, and meadows. With this mentality, it's hard to imagine that city dwellers can connect to nature in the urban environments in which they live. This simply is not the case! Altering the lens through which you view experiences in diverse, bustling cities can lead to an explosion of nature discovery that was once overlooked.

The biggest misconception is that green spaces are needed to connect with nature. Although they help, true nature connection starts with simply opening your senses, slowing down, and becoming more aware. Feel the ground beneath your feet, look at the sky overhead, and notice how the weather feels on your skin.

Practice using a keen eye and spotting signs of life in your neighborhood. These opportunities are everywhere: plants grow in cracks and crevices, moss grows on sidewalks and buildings, insects may be scurrying underfoot! Encourage children to engage with the nature that you discover. Perhaps they would like to start a nature collection: stones, pine needles, leaves, berries—what will you discover in your neighborhood? Add to your community by potting plants into containers. Research what native plants will attract pollinators and help out the local ecosystem while you're at it!

Children learn best through play. When children have time to actively explore their environment, they learn how the world works. When they have opportunities to freely engage with nature, their imaginations run wild. Found objects such as rocks, sticks, leaves, dirt, and puddles provide open-ended props for play. For example, let's explore all the ways a child may learn when playing freely in a puddle: they may explore the early concepts of density when they see a leaf float but a stone sink, or learn how to gauge depth by seeing how far a stick will go when inserted, or see how waves travel when watching ripples. When children get the opportunities to freely learn and play in nature, it leads to increased comfort in spending time outdoors, creating a lifelong connection to the natural world.

The best way parents can nurture unstructured engagement with nature is to simply let children play. Set clear boundaries to ensure safety but try not to limit children's interactions. Children *everywhere* deserve opportunities to get dirty, be curious, and cultivate a relationship with the natural world.

INDIGENOUS PERSPECTIVES

SALLY ANDERSON, MA, DIRECTOR AND LEAD EDUCATOR

Sol Forest School, Tijeras, New Mexico

What are some appropriate ways parents can include indigenous perspectives with respect to exploring the landscape?

Although forest and nature schools are enjoying a surge the world over, indigenous people have been offering meaningful, land-based education to their children for millennia. Native American approaches to education (and countless other indigenous cultures) emphasize experiential learning and peer-to-peer learning and require people to take responsibility for their own learning. Nature play creates a similar experience because this type of play is experiential and typically child led, allowing the child to take responsibility for what they are learning.

With at least 15,000 years of intellectual and cultural traditions, oral stories, and educational experience on our lands, knowing something about Native American perspective on education, as well Native American history and culture in your "neck of the woods" can bring a deeper understanding of the place you inhabit. In turn, sharing this knowledge with your children will allow them to create a deeper respect for and sense of place.

There are several ways to include indigenous people and/or perspectives with respect to exploring the landscapes where you live. The first and most obvious is to reach out to indigenous communities, if there are communities near you. In New Mexico, there is a diverse indigenous population of over twenty tribes. To me, it is my moral obligation to know a little bit about the people who inhabited this majestic land long before I did. In relation to my work running a forest school, I have made it a point to invite local Native leaders to our opening day each year. They bless the site we use for communal gatherings and confer a blessing for the school year over our children and families. Oral stories, anecdotes, and songs are shared, as well as kid-friendly activities, a potluck, and lots of conversation and laughter. This day serves to ground us in place while also reminding us that we are all more similar than different, and that we all live under the same sun.

If there are not indigenous groups in your area to visit or reach out to, you can visit a museum and/or cultural landmarks to learn about the people who had originally inhabited the place you call home. You can also set an intention to read Native American stories and legends to your children, especially those coming from people with a history linked to your location. Most North American indigenous tribes are deeply connected to viewing life through the Four Directions. This philosophical view of the world is deeply Earth-based and therefore connected to the land and the environment. It tells us about who we are as human beings; a balanced person is composed of a well-developed emotional, physical, spiritual, and intellectual self. Parenting through this lens, with a focus on your child's four directions of development (emotional, physical, spiritual, and intellectual), is a holistic approach to child-rearing akin to the approach taken in many indigenous communities.

Finally, you can make a point of educating your children about Native peoples and their lands. Native people have never forgotten that we belong to the Earth (not the other way around) and sharing these stories of struggle will help grow children who have empathy for other humans, as well as empathy for our earth.

We don't inherit the earth from our ancestors, we borrow it from our children.

—Unknown

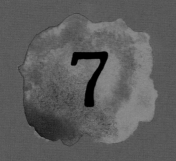

7

TEMPLATES

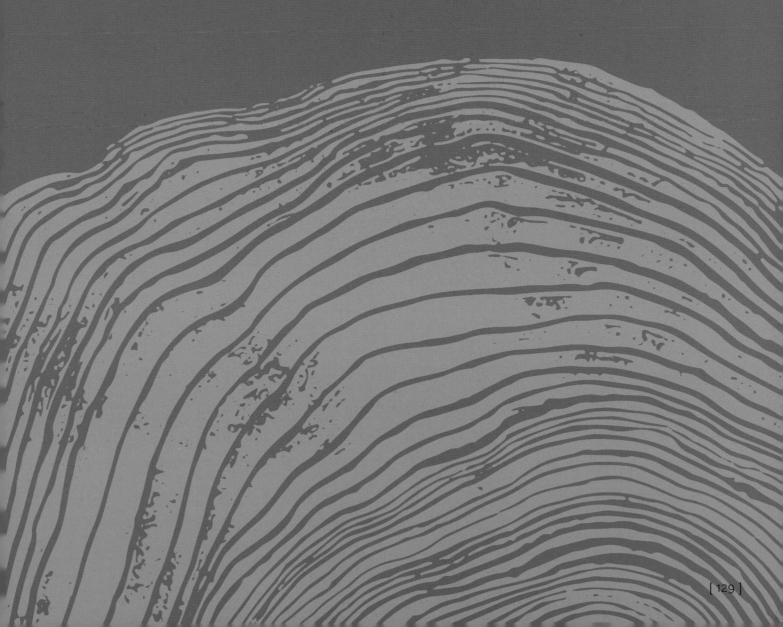

NATURAL EVENTS CALENDAR (YEARLY)

Use this page to record significant natural events you observe throughout the year. It may be useful to note dates, times, locations, species information, and comparisons from previous years. For more detailed documentation, use the monthly calendar template.

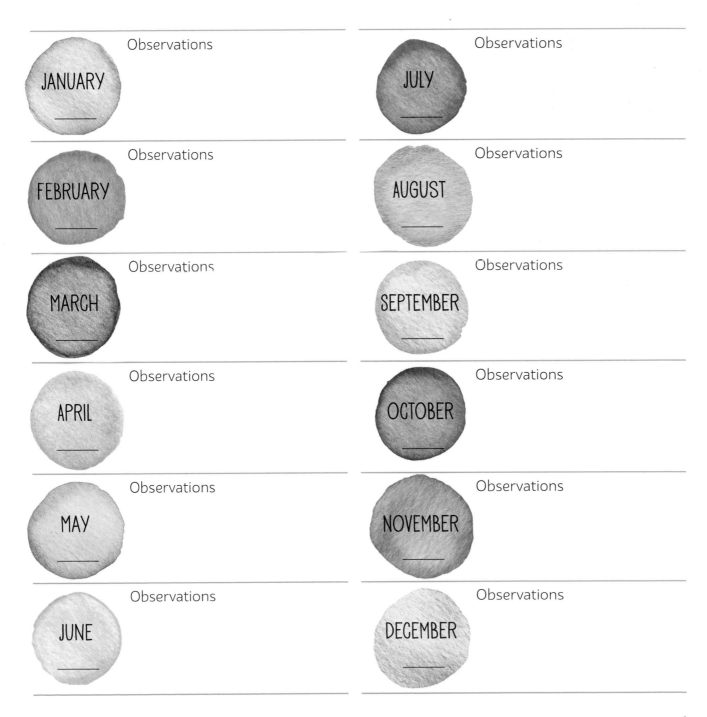

JANUARY — Observations

FEBRUARY — Observations

MARCH — Observations

APRIL — Observations

MAY — Observations

JUNE — Observations

JULY — Observations

AUGUST — Observations

SEPTEMBER — Observations

OCTOBER — Observations

NOVEMBER — Observations

DECEMBER — Observations

NATURAL EVENTS CALENDAR (MONTHLY)

Use this page to record significant natural events you observe each month. First, fill in the month, year, and dates below. Note times, locations, species information, daily temperature, weather, Moon phase, and comparisons from previous years to make a detailed record of nature events.

 MONTH

 YEAR

Sunday	Monday	Tuesday	Wednesday	Thursday	Friday	Saturday

MOON JOURNAL

Use this page to track the phases of the Moon during a 28-day lunar cycle. Label each day, then make nightly observations of the Moon. Draw a picture of the Moon with a white colored pencil, crayon, or white piece of chalk in the space below. Make notes of other astronomical events such as planets or stars you see in your Natural Events Calendar.

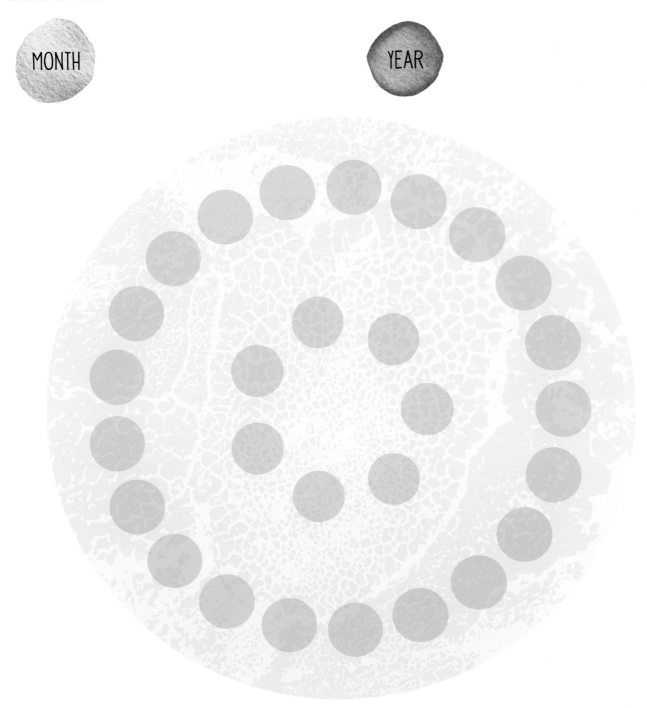

MONTH

YEAR

NATURE IN THE CITY SCAVENGER HUNT

Nature is everywhere! Go for a walk to explore nature. Can you find the items below?

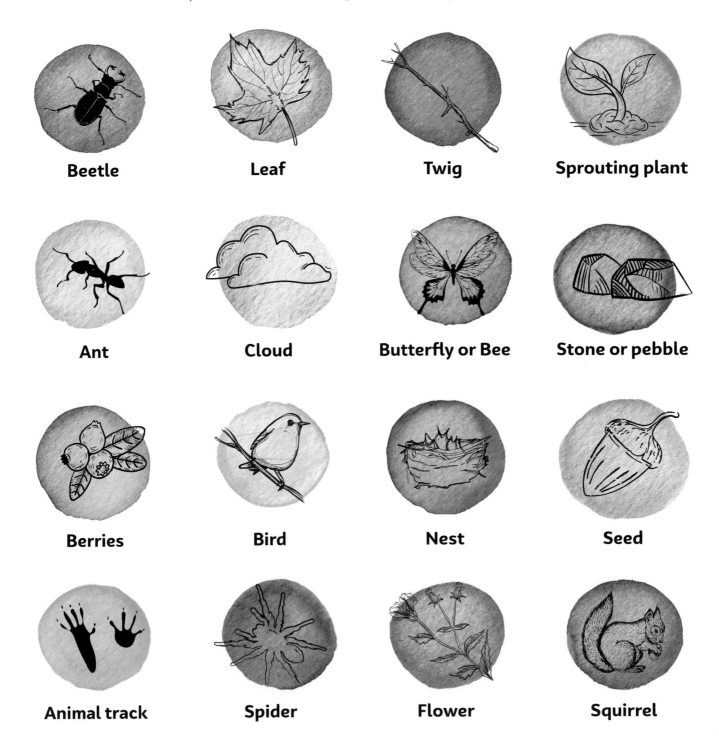

Beetle

Leaf

Twig

Sprouting plant

Ant

Cloud

Butterfly or Bee

Stone or pebble

Berries

Bird

Nest

Seed

Animal track

Spider

Flower

Squirrel

SEEDLING GROWTH CHART

Track the growth of your seedlings and watch them grow! Use this chart to record measurements of each plant or draw what they look like. Which do you think will grow fastest?

Name of Plant _____ | Planting Date _____

WEEK 1 Date:

WEEK 2 Date:

WEEK 3 Date:

WEEK 4 Date:

WEEK 5 Date:

WEEK 6 Date:

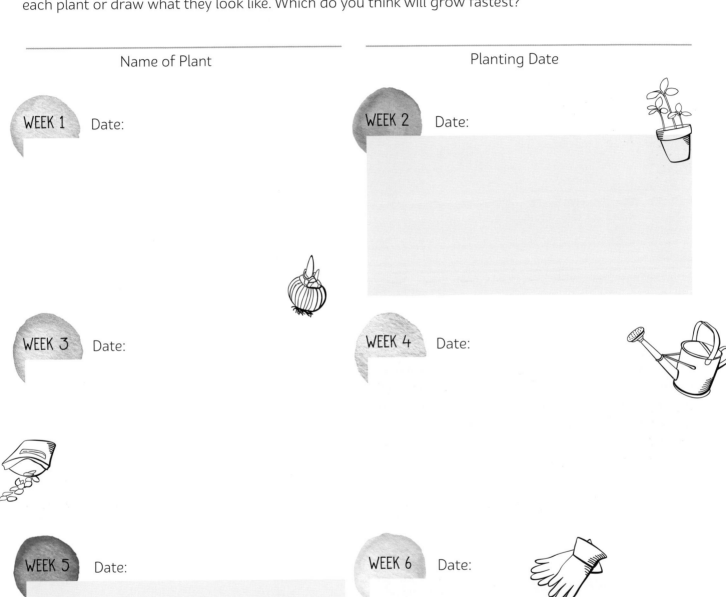

RESOURCES

SELECT RESOURCES

Natural History

Amphibians

Frog Watch, www.aza.org/frogwatch

Astronomy

Sky and Telescope, www.skyandtelescope.com/astronomy-information

Bees

Xerces Society, www.xerces.org

The Honeybee Conservancy, www.thehoneybeeconservancy.org

Birds

The Cornell Lab of Ornithology, www.allaboutbirds.org

Migratory Bird Treaty Act, U.S. Fish and Wildlife Service, www.fws.gov/birds/policies-and-regulations/laws-legislations/migratory-bird-treaty-act.php

Butterflies

Butterfly Conservation, www.butterfly-conservation.org

Geology

USGS, www.usgs.gov/faqs/can-you-identify-my-rock-or-mineral

Insects, general

www.bugguide.net

Mushrooms and Fungus

North American Mycological Association, www.namyco.org

Processing Natural Clay

www.practicalprimitive.com/skillofthemonth/processingclay.html

Tracking

www.naturetracking.com

Plant Identification

Arbor Day Foundation, www.arborday.org

Wild Edible, www.wildedible.com/foraging#sustainability

Weather and Wildlife

National Geographic Society, www.nationalgeographic.org

Smithsonian Institution, www.smithsonian.com

www.smithsonianmag.com/science-nature/the-whispering-trees-180968084

Nature Play and Outdoor Learning

Children & Nature Network, www.childrenandnature.org

Eastern Region Association of Forest and Nature Schools, www.erafans.org

Free Forest School, www.freeforestschool.org

National Wildlife Federation, www.nwf.org/en/Kids-and-Family/Connecting-Kids-and-Nature/Nature-Play-Spaces

National Association for the Education of Young Children, www.naeyc.org

Natural Start Alliance, www.naturalstart.org

Nature Explore Program, Dimensions Educational Research Foundation, www.natureexplore.org

North American Association for Environmental Education, www.naaee.org

Wilder Child, www.wilderchild.com

SELECTED CHILDREN'S BOOKS

Berger, M. (2003). *Spinning Spiders*. HarperCollins: New York, NY.

Bradley, K. (2019). *Easy Peasy: Gardening for Kids*. Little Gestalten.

Davies, N. (2012). *Outside Your Window: A First Book of Nature*.

Davies, N. (2004). *Bat Loves the Night*.

Dendy, L. (1996). *Tracks, Scats and Signs: Take Along Guide*.

Gray, R. (2014). *Have You Heard the Nesting Bird?*

Hawthorne, L. (2019). *The Night Flower*.

Higgins, K. (2018). *Everything You Need for a Treehouse*.

Ingoglia, G. (2013). *The Tree Book for Kids and Their Grown-ups*.

Knowlton, L. (2017). *Maple Syrup from the Sugarhouse*.

Kohara, K. (2011). *Here Comes Jack Frost*.

Lloyd, M. W. (2016). *Finding Wild*.

Messner, K. (2017). *Up In the Garden and Down In the Dirt*.

McKenna Siddals, M. (2014). *Compost Stew: An A to Z Recipe for the Earth*.

Pak, K. (2016). *Goodbye Summer, Hello Autumn*.

Pfeffer, W. (2007). *A Log's Life*.

Portis, A. (2007). *Not a Stick*.

Preston-Gannon, F. (2019). *By the Light of the Moon*.

Schaefer, L. and A. Schaefer (2016). *Because of an Acorn*.

Swanson, S. (2008). *To Be Like the Sun*.

Wagner Lloyd, M. (2017). *Fort-Building Time*.

Ward, J. and L. Falkenstern. (2009). *The Busy Tree*

CONTRIBUTORS

Sally Anderson
Director and Lead Educator
Sol Forest School
Tijeras, New Mexico

Yash Bhagwanji
Associate Professor
Early Childhood Education
    Florida Atlantic University
Boca Raton, Florida

Lauren Brown
Founding Director
Asheville Farmstead School
Candler, North Carolina

Peter Dargatz
Kindergarten Teacher
Woodside Elementary School
Sussex, Wisconsin

Monica French
Cofounder and Director
Wild Haven Forest Preschool
    and Childcare
Baltimore, Maryland

Patricia Leon
Program Director,
Parent and Child Institute
    Miami Nature Playschool
North Miami, Florida

Beth Savitz
Head of Parent and Child Programs
Irvine Nature Center
Owings Mills, Maryland

Marisa Soboleski
Forest School Program Director
New Mexico School for the Deaf
Santa Fe and Albuquerque, New Mexico

Paige Vonder Haar
Director
Bunnell House Early
    Childhood Lab School
Fairbanks, Alaska

Sheila Williams Ridge
Director
Shirley G. Moore Lab
School Institute of Child Development,
    University of Minnesota
Minneapolis, Minnesota

Susie Wirth
Outreach Director (retired)
Arbor Day Foundation and
    Dimensions Foundation
Omaha, Nebraska

ABOUT THE AUTHORS

Karen Madigan has worked closely with children, families, and fellow educators for over twenty-five years. She is a beloved educator at Irvine Nature Center in Maryland, where she was instrumental in establishing The Nature Preschool. Karen believes that all children deserve fresh air, sunshine, and tree hugs. She is excited to share this book with fellow teachers and families in the hopes that it will inspire them to embrace the wonders of nature and invite them to play and learn in the best classroom of all, outdoors!

Monica Wiedel-Lubinski is a passionate advocate for nature-based education. She began her professional journey as a naturalist where she developed programs for nearly two decades, including The Nature Preschool at Irvine Nature Center. She is currently the director of the Eastern Region Association of Forest and Nature Schools (ERAFANS), which builds capacity for equitable nature-based education through professional development. In an effort to expand nature-based learning opportunities in her local community, she also cofounded Wild Haven Forest Preschool (2017) and Notchcliff Nature Preschool at Glen Meadows Retirement Community (2019). As an author, keynote presenter, and consultant, Monica lends expertise to people creating nature-based schools and natural play spaces wherever she goes. Monica holds a bachelor's degree in art education and a master's degree in early childhood education from Towson University in Baltimore, Maryland.

INDEX